To t... [illegible]
D. Lasugow family
God Bless you
Pastor E. Hope
8/7/2007
Mark 9:23

The Hand OF THE LORD

Was Upon Me

Ezekiel 37:1

CLARENCE W. HOPSON

The Hand
OF THE LORD
Was Upon Me

Clarence W. Hopson

ISBN 1-891773-35-6

Printed in the United States of America

Published by Orman Press Inc.
4200 Sandy Lake Drive
Lithonia, Georgia 30038
(770) 808-0999
(770) 808-1955 (fax)
www.ormanpress.com

CONTENTS

ENDORSEMENT

Dr. Clarence W. Hopson has written a book that is a must read for every pastor and believer. It has been rightfully said that experience is the best teacher. However, it is even more advantageous and much less painful to learn from the experience of others. Pastors, both young and seasoned, can learn from this book. Also, if the reader can grasp the panoramic view of the Clarence Hopson Ministry, they will be blessed with a unique and beneficial model of doing church that is designed to worship God and God alone, a model worthy of duplication in any church setting and culture.

The book is appropriately titled *The Hand of The Lord Was Upon Me*. Dr. Hopson traces his footsteps from his humble beginnings in rural Mississippi, with an infusion of incidents and experiences where the hand of the Lord was upon him, to his present position as pastor of the rapidly growing Broadview Baptist Church in Broadview, Illinois. In addition, he shares the vision of the future Broadview Baptist Church.

The Hand of The Lord Was Upon Me is more than an autobiography of a blessed man of God, it is also a documentation of the goodness of God in the life of a successful pastor's ministry in the history of a church. Therefore, the book will be enjoyable to every believer. Moreover, the book could be given to nonbelievers as an evangelistic aid. I simply enjoyed reading the book, although it was also a learning experience for me.

I am blessed to personally know the author. (It is one thing to be able to recite the 23rd Psalm ["The Lord is my Shepherd"], but it is a greater thing to know the Shepherd.) I have a bonding relationship with the undershepherd, Pastor Hopson, and his wife, First Lady Anne Hopson. Pastor Hopson is a man of God with the highest of integrity. His branches are overloaded with the Fruit of the Spirit. He is the only man I have ever known that can not only disagree without being disagreeable, but can disagree and appear to be agreeable. I can witness to the truth that the "hand of the Lord" has indeed been upon Dr. Clarence W. Hopson. It is without hesitation that I recommend this book.

All who read this book will be encouraged and especially blessed.

Pastor George O. McCalep, Jr., Ph.D.
President/CEO of Orman Press, Inc.
Lithonia, Georgia

FOREWORD

Dear Friend,

Pastor Clarence Hopson is a giant in the ministry, and I am so happy that he passed along his life testimony and his wisdom. When I speak of his wisdom, I don't mean words of wisdom for meeting particular circumstances, though there are many of those insights. I mean primarily the overarching recognition that the Lord's hand is upon those who seek and obey him. The book is saturated with that great wisdom.

Some ministers are inclined to compromise their calling out of fear, greed, or ambition. Not so with Clarence Hopson. He has kept his eye on the Lord and his Word, asking at every turn whether things were pleasing to Him. The result has been a chain of miracles and a life of gratitude. This book is a treasury of those accounts of God's blessing.

Pastor Hopson is careful to trace the way in which the Lord has prepared him in advance for the range of challenges he would face later on in the ministry. He has a very strong sense of the sovereignty and providence of God. From his earliest days in Mississippi through his Army service, his move to work in Chicago, and his growth as a servant of the Lord in Melrose Park, Clarence saw God shape him perfectly for the work at Broadview. And, of course, he thanks God for his wonderful wife and family, who have walked with him through the years.

I wish young pastors would read this account of a man who has attended to the great things of God with keen focus on evangelism and discipleship. I have seen the splendid ministers emerging from his ministry and his gifted interaction with seminary students. But I also think that veteran pastors will find fellowship, encouragement, and even counsel in this book.

As much as I appreciate his writing, I even more appreciate the man, a dear friend in the ministry. He has been instrumental in church planting in a variety of ways and continues as a strong elder brother in the Lord. I commend his words and example to you.

Sincerely,

Mark Coppenger, Pastor
Evanston Baptist Church
Evanston, IL

ACKNOWLEDGMENTS

First, let me acknowledge my beloved wife, Annie Hopson, who has stood by my side, not only during the writing of this book, but also throughout our nearly half century of married life. She has given me much needed constructive criticism and made me give serious thought to my writings. I thank her so much and appreciate her continuous support.

I also want to acknowledge Priscilla Rule, Broadview Baptist Church clerk, who kept excellent church records, which enabled me to put things together so that I could share with you, the reader, what the Lord has done for us in this local fellowship.

Brother Marion Morris is to be acknowledged for his information and recall of the many blessings that occurred in the Broadview family while he was with us. He went to be with the Lord before this book was published, but he was a great contributor.

Dr. Leon Thompson, along with Brother Morris, was with us for our transition from the original location to this location on 17th Avenue in 1980. Dr. Thompson's input was particularly helpful in the Christian Education area.

I would also like to thank Mary Meredith who did the painstaking job of proofreading this entire manuscript.

Finally, I would like to acknowledge Eugenia L. Curry, who did most of the transcribing, editing, and rewriting of the manuscript. In fact, it was she who insisted that we go forward when I was ready to turn back because of the many things that I was involved in. I am grateful that during the interview process she prodded my memory and brought back things I had not thought about for a very long time. I certainly want to thank her for perseverance and insistence in the writing of this book.

The instances cited in this book where I stated that God had his hand on me were just highlights of my many experiences where the matchless power of God was shown.

May God keep you. I hope that the writings in this book are a great inspiration to others who are struggling to be what God wants them to be. May God bless you, in Jesus' name.

Pastor Clarence W. Hopson
Broadview Baptist Church
Broadview, Il

INTRODUCTION

It is my fondest desire that this book will be used as a teaching tool, not only for students, but also by young ministers and/or pastors. I want the reader to see the far-reaching and consistent hand of the Lord upon His creation.

The basic theme throughout this book is to point out various situations when the Lord's hand was upon me during the different stages of my life as a child, teen, military man, new husband, evangelist and pastor.

I have lived through some of the greatest eras of progress in man's history. The horse and buggy were still in style when I was born, though cars were also being used. My cousin had a very fancy buggy with special wheels. Coming home from school, I would see them. The buggy is a striking contrast to the technologically equipped automobiles and 747's that we now use for transportation.

I had a wonderful childhood. I was neither poverty-stricken nor did I come from a single parent household. These are not prerequisites for God to use you. He can and He does use individuals with this kind of background, though this background is not necessary.

The purpose of this book is not only to share my life story, but also to show that the hand of the Lord was upon me. My inspiration for writing this book evolved after looking back on my life and noting that even though I was raised in rural Mississippi, when segregation was practiced openly and legally, the Lord protected me and preserved me from death.

I hope information in this book will be passed on to the next generation. I especially want it to be a blessing for and benefit to students and new preachers of the gospel, so that they will know that when God's able hand is upon you, you will succeed.

CHAPTER 1

BEGINNINGS

"Before I formed thee in the belly I knew thee;
and before thou camest forth out of the womb I sanctified thee,
and I ordained thee a prophet unto the nations."
Jeremiah 1:5

I can still smell the wonderful odors in our house at Christmas time. There would be apples, oranges, nuts, and lots of peppermint candies all through the house. My mother filled drawers with homemade chocolate, coconut and caramel cakes, and sweet potato and apple pies. She stored them all in the safe, a large wooden cabinet made with air holes to keep the wonderful homemade baked goods from spoiling.

I get goose bumps thinking of my rich childhood Christmases surrounded by family and friends. The entertainment was the gathering of friends and neighbors around the wood fireplace, telling stories about various things—sometimes, ghost stories. My mother would have bowls full of teacakes for the guests stored on top of the safe. Teacakes are similar to our butter cookies, but larger and thicker.

Our family was blessed with lots of children and I was very mischievous. Because we were small children and could not see on top of the safe, we stood tiptoed to reach the cookies. We would keep going back again and again to get one of the scrumptious teacakes. By the time the guests arrived, there would be none left. I'm sure my mother knew what we were doing; she might have even put them there for us knowing what we would do.

Many times my parents had friends over. The women would quilt, and the men would make lamps with coal oil and rags. They were quite ingenious.

The quilts were made in a communal setting. When winter came, the whole community had enough quilts to keep their families warm. Beautiful quilts were made and given to new brides as wedding presents.

I was born to Mr. and Mrs. Fred Hopson, Sr. on May 27, 1928, in Bolton, Mississippi. Bolton is about 30 miles from Jackson, the state capitol. I am the fourth child of ten. My parents had eight sons and two daughters.

Even though my father was born in the 1800's and my mother in the early 1900's, they could both read and write. This was very important during that time because most Blacks did not possess these skills because of slavery. They were both devout Christians. Christ was always honored in our home. When the church was too far away for us to travel physically during the week for prayer meeting, we would have family devotions at home, which included singing, praying and studying the Bible. We sang old beloved songs. One of my favorites was and is "It Will Be Glory." My father never made us go to church. We went because we grew up with the Christian influence in our home. Usually, children will follow their parents' lead. It is much easier to lead by example than by oratory.

Since I was the fourth oldest and we were all boys, I was the houseboy who always helped my mother. I was the Jacob of the Hopson clan. My early life was carefree, even though segregation was practiced openly in Mississippi. Because I was a black person in Mississippi, I knew that displaying intelligence made me a threat to the white man. My father taught us that no one was better than we were; neither were we better than anyone else. Consequently, I grew up without any feelings of inferiority. The Lord shielded us.

I was born during the Depression, a time when clever farming was essential. My father was a highly skilled farmer. His side of the family were never slaves. My father's grandfather was a Native American who married a Black woman. Because my father was such an excellent farmer, we always had plenty to eat. We also hunted in winter and fished in summer so we had plenty of fresh game. My father raised our hogs for sausage and butchered cows for beefsteak. My mother used a pound press, to press butter. We had plenty of milk and cream from the cows. We would churn the fresh milk, and from the cream that was on top of the milk, we would get our butter, all of which was readily shared with the community. Everyone in the community had plenty to eat and shared. So, when our neighbors butchered cows or hogs, we shared in their bounty. We didn't have many clothes, but had plenty of food. We did all the processing. I fed cattle, hogs, and chickens and gathered eggs. When we were young, we were not aware of the danger of segregation. I could have been killed on many occasions because of my attitude and actions. But I was unaware of this; surely the hand of the Lord was upon me. God can and does make your enemies behave. Praise God!!!

My mother's maiden name was Pecolia Thomas. There were clans of Hopsons, Hills, Thomases and Clays living in this particular section of the village of Bolton. We were like a village within a village. The white people did not tell us when or where to go, and this gave us a kind of freedom. We did not mix with the whites. We knew there was a demarcation between Whites and Blacks, but we felt safe in our domain. Many of us were property owners, and this gave us even more freedom.

In reference to inferiority complexes, during the Depression, many people came through our community, and we gave them food to help them along. Many of these people were Whites who had come seeking food. My dad was always a generous person and, as I've stated, a good farmer. He often gave food to these poor travelers. Since many of them were white, uneducated, poor, hungry and had to come to us for help, that erased any thoughts I might have entertained as to my being inferior. I thought we were better than they were because we had to give to them. When they had departed, my parents would say negative things about them, and we would repeat these things. That is why it is critically important for parents to be careful what they say around their children.

My father was the youngest of 14 children. He had a sister who recently died at over 100 years of age. I only knew two of my uncles, my father's brothers, Richard and Ervin. I last saw my uncle Ervin in 1972. My brother and I visited him then. Later on in that same year, we also buried him.

Changes were evident in the South in 1972. This time, we stayed in the Tupelo Holiday Inn because segregation had been abolished. As I said, I enjoyed my childhood. I started to school when I was six years old.

15

There was no kindergarten for Blacks in those days in the State of Mississippi. I started in pre-primer. The book used in pre-primer had a soft cover. The book and the grade were both called the pre-primer. We would study this soft-cover book all year. This book was a beginner reader book. I could sing it by the end of the year. That is how I became an excellent reader.

When I was seven years old, I was promoted to primer. The primer was a hardback book. When I became eight I was promoted to the 1st grade. That is how I completed eight years of schooling by age 16. I became very proficient in spelling, math, reading and geography. That was the way the system was set up then. I continued going to school through the grade system, and by the time I was 16, I had completed grade school. I should have been a junior in high school. However, completing the 8th grade then was comparable to completing high school now. I know because years later, when I came to Chicago and applied for a job with Northern Illinois Gas Company during the Civil Rights Movement Era, I scored extremely high on the test; the personnel staff member made a remark about my score in light of my total years of formal education. He had difficulty understanding why I was 16 years old and had only completed grade school. I had to explain the system to him.

A classmate of mine who came to Chicago from this system during WWII, was put back a grade because he was from Mississippi. However, because he was so proficient in math, reading, spelling, geography, etc., he was later advanced a level. We did fractions for fun on Fridays at school. Math was natural for us because of the teaching styles of our instructors.

When I was in Mississippi, we had a two-room schoolhouse. This school had only two teachers. One teacher taught grades pre-primer to fifth; the other teacher taught grades six, seven, and eight. During that time, it was a rule that you got a whipping if you did not get your lessons completed. There were no parents coming to the school to reprimand the teachers, but rather the parents would come to reprimand their children for disobeying their teachers. I loved school and learning. I did not miss a day. The teachers kept their students motivated. For instance, in our history class, the instructor would make the announcement, "We are going to Japan tomorrow," if

16

we were going to be studying about Japan that next day. I could hardly wait to take my trip to Japan via the pages of my history book. My teacher's name was Mrs. Thomas. I was called the "teacher's pet." I have always been comfortable with the ladies. Remember, I was the houseboy at home and around my mother a lot. Occasionally I would invite the teacher home for dinner, with my parents' permission, of course.

Mrs. Bessie Griffin, the senior teacher, had foresight. She taught us how to read water meters and electric meters from our textbooks because she knew we might become city dwellers later on. I visited both Mrs. Griffin and Miss Thomas when I became an adult and told them how much I appreciated them and the things they taught me about life from which I greatly benefited.

Before we went to school, my mother would cook a big breakfast. She cooked as if she were cooking for a restaurant. I would have plenty to eat. We had syrup, butter and middling (bacon) during the week and biscuits, syrup and chicken on Sundays. Since the middling had the skin still attached when it was sliced, you ate the meat and chewed the skin. It could last for quite a while. I ate fast because I was raised with a large group of children. My mother never bothered us about the quantity of food we ate or the pace at which we ate. We were very active physically and burned off all those calories through farm work.

We used to go hunting and fishing. We knew how to gather the fruit that was edible, i.e., pecans, persimmons, watermelons, sorghum cane and sugar cane. We made molasses twice a year. We would make the syrup with a horse pulling a long tree pole that squeezed the juice from the cane into vats for cooking. I understood all this; I knew how to survive. I had a sense of belonging. I had no peer pressure. We hunted for birds, rabbits and other wild game using our slingshots. We raised sorghum and sugar cane. Sorghum was gathered in August; we gathered sugar cane in the fall.

We were just as mischievous as we could be. We would go out and eat cane from the cane fields and watermelons from the watermelon patch and hide the leftovers. We did not have to steal from our parents; they would have given it to us, but it was more fun stealing it. *Proverbs 9:17* says, "Stolen waters are sweet and bread eaten in secret is pleasant." The reader should be aware that I am not condoning stealing, but merely recording something that occurred.

Several people made syrup. They sold, gave, or bartered some to other families. We had a good carefree life gathering the various foods for our winter's survival. My mother canned fruits and vegetables for the winter. I assisted her.

My brothers and I would go swimming. I didn't know how to swim. I would have one foot stuck in the mud and splash the water with the other. My brothers, who could swim and knew I was only making noise, threatened me. We went to the blue hole (a small creek-like body of water that was too deep for my toes to reach the bottom) and my brothers said, "If you don't stretch out and swim we will sink you." So, I stretched out. I learned that when I stretched out I could swim. That is how it works with God; you have to stretch out and trust in his Word. God's hand was upon me. I learned to swim when I stretched out in faith. This was a valuable lesson for me to learn for my life and ministry.

We also took corn to the mill to make meal; the mill tender took part of the corn for himself, and he ground the other part for us. We took eggs to town for selling and bartering. This was a common practice among the people of the community.

Seeing the animals mate and give birth were invaluable experiences for me. This ritual was a natural process to children who were raised on farms. They knew when the hogs, cows, and horses were giving birth. Children would sometimes accompany parents during the mating and birthing activities of various animals. This has many advantages over reading it in books.

Going to the grocery store was almost unheard of. We went to town to buy oil and flour. We got lard (a form of cooking oil) from the hogs. We bought flour in 100 pound sacks. We hung meat up in the smoke house to be cured and preserved for future use. We had pork crackling (fat trimmings) which was the skin that remained after we made lard. My mother took the crackling pieces of meat and made crackling bread. I went fishing and hunting whenever I got ready. I learned to handle and respect firearms as a child because my father trained all of us to use them properly.

I had a very comfortable life in our three-bedroom home. There were two large beds in each bedroom. My mother and father slept in one room. There were four beds for the children. We slept two or three children in each bed. I still sleep on the edge of the bed. All of us were not at home at the same time. I am the youngest of the first group of four. In other words, some of the younger children were home after I left.

My parents must have sensed leadership ability in me when I was a child because they trusted me with many areas of responsibility far beyond my age level. For instance, when my mother went visiting and knew it was going to be dark when she returned, she took me to escort her because she said I was unafraid. This gave me confidence. My aunt, who is now 80+ years old, gave me my first babysitting job at age six. Being six years old with that kind of responsibility, I must have had the ability to distinguish right from wrong. I would start the fire in the wood stove when I saw her coming home. I could change the baby's diapers when she was in the field working with her husband. This distinguished me from all the other children. When I returned home from my aunt's house after the summer months, my brothers and sisters greeted me with honor as if I were a guest; they do so even to this day. I am a kind of Joseph to our family. Truly, the hand of the Lord was upon me.

The next year, I repeated the babysitting cycle with another uncle in a different county. My uncle's wife was a young woman, as naive as she could be; she trusted me to carry her baby across a blue hole (creek), which was very deep, and we had to cross using a two-foot wide plank. If I had fallen in, we both would have died. The Holy Spirit guided us; we were both crazy and the baby didn't know.

I went to church with them each Sunday. It was customary for the parishioners to sell ice cream and food on the church grounds. We had a Spirit filled service and homemade ice cream after service. I was enjoying my newfound chores as a sitter away from home and my childhood all at the same time; it was a real learning experience and very fulfilling for me. This gave me more and more confidence, as I grew older.

I liked to pick cotton; it was my favorite farming chore. I could pick 200 to 300 pounds of cotton and have time to spare. We worked for the white farmers for extra money, which we could use to go to the movies in town. This was in addition to the work that we did on our own family farm. We owned horses. When we played cowboys, we had the real horses. This is when I first learned that horses are easily trained. Whatever we saw the cowboys do in the movies with their horses, we would come home and try it with real horses. That's why I do not care anything about horseback riding today. I have had enough of that to last me for a lifetime. I had a wonderful carefree life.

We lived near the Big Black River in Mississippi. I was always afraid of water, even though I could swim. The water would back up to where we could see it in the woods way beyond its banks. It always frightened me. The farmers could go fishing and hunting, and they would be able to catch more prey because the water backed up. So there was no shortage of good meats for consumption.

As I said, when I was a child, I was very mischievous, and many funny things seemed to happen to me. I remember one time I struck a match in a straw field, and the field caught fire and burned like mad. My father knew I'd done it, but he did not whip me for it. He and our neighbor had to fight to put the fire out. There was no fire department.

It was so interesting for me as a child to see my parents make provisions for us, such as using lye to make hominy corn, and watching my mother prepare rice. Rice smelled so good to me when it was cooking, but unlike my brothers, I disliked both rice and hominy corn. My father plowed and planted many different kinds of food plants. This was during the Great Depression, and as an adult, I have met many people who talk about their lack of food back then. But I don't remember ever being hungry, or having nothing to eat. We had various vegetables and fruits. Our father was a great provider for his family.

As I look back on my life, I enjoyed going to church with my parents and my aunt and uncle. Once, when I was spending time with my aunt and uncle, they went to town and bought me some tennis shoes. I had these new tennis shoes but they hurt my feet badly. They burned my feet. My uncle took me outside of the church and cut my shoes to shreds giving me some relief while my aunt continued singing inside the church. My feet felt aflame, but this was one of the fondest memories of my early life.

There was a minister named Jack Walker who had been sent down South from the North to teach and preach to black people. He was a great teacher and preacher. I remember his telling us as children how every tick of the clock brings one closer to one's end. As I recall at age seven I could preach word for word what he said. Rev. Jack Walker would preach a symbolic sermon saying, "God had two horses; one was named Tornado and one was named Cyclone." I would go home and preach the chicken's funeral, and the little girls would shout like the women they had seen at church. I would say what I heard the preacher say at church, word for word.

One thing that stood out about this minister of the gospel was that he always encouraged children. He would ask us "What are you going to be in life?" He would come to the Sunday School class and have a chat with us. This example was a great help to me in my ministry as I taught and witnessed to young people. You need to chat with and listen to children. You need to show them that you are interested in their lives Children grow up and they will remember you for the way you treated them when they were small. That is why I am careful how I treat everyone, because we do reap what we sow. *(Galatians 6:7)*

The first preacher that I remember coming to our home was Rev. Curtis West. He was my parent's pastor. He pastored the Orange Hill Missionary Baptist Church at that time. Years later, I was baptized at that church. The pastor at the time of my conversion was Rev. Lamar Robinson. When you were on the mourners bench, the leaders would ask you who would you like to pray for your salvation.

Jack Irvin, an evangelist, preached a sermon that I remember to this very day. In later years I understood it as a parable. (It was preached when my oldest brother, Fred, got saved.) The sermon went as follows: There was a snake and the snake bit the maid. The farmer took his gun to kill it but the snake spit up copper until it pleased the man. Then he bit his daughter, but he spit up gold and it pleased the man. Then he came in and bit his wife. The farmer got his gun and the snake spit up diamonds.

Each time the man would not kill the snake, for he benefited from what he got from the snake. The next time he came in to get the farmer and the farmer protested, "I saved you." But, said the snake, "You knew I was a snake." The preacher would vary his voice inflection and pitch as he told this story, and his belly would shake. Some of the sinners would be outside the church building listening to the sermon. The sinners would get saved inside and outside of the church. I learned from this parable that we are not to delay in doing what we need to do to be saved. The scripture says that "the day you hear my voice, harden not your heart" *(Hebrews 3:15)*. The moral of the story was that if one puts off making Christ his Savior, he would be lost and I understood that. This is why the preacher should preach the Word of God without fear. The Word of God is still "more powerful and sharper than any two edged sword" *(Hebrews 4:12)*. This is what was instilled into me in my early life, and that's why the Hand of the Lord was upon me to obey him by faith.

I was very cognizant of what the adults said and did and what my environment was imparting. That is why I know the hand of the Lord was upon me when I look back and reflect over my past.

CHAPTER 2

CONVERSION

"Therefore if any man be in Christ, he is a new creature..."
II Cor. 5:17a

I had my conversion experience, that is, I accepted Jesus Christ as my personal savior at age 13. During this period in history, we had what we called "mourners benches." These were the first benches in front of the church sanctuary directly in front of the pulpit. The unsaved persons were seated there so they could hear the preacher clearly and they got on their knees during various prayers as they heard the preacher offer the message of salvation. Deciding whether or not you were really serious, the congregation required that you must "get in earnest," i.e., be godly sorry for your sins, be repentant, and want Christ to be the head of your life. Not only would you concentrate on asking God to forgive you for your sins and ask him to come into your life, but also, you would go around the congregation and ask certain strong Christians to pray for you. They called being saved "getting religion."

When the church service ended, the mourners (those sinners on the front mourner's bench) were allowed to go out first, and concentrate on praying. I know all of this is not necessary now, but it certainly made one sincere about what one wanted to do.

I went out into the woods to pray. Being alone and concentrating was important. I was "in earnest." I remember it as if it were yesterday when the Holy Spirit was poured out on me. It is a presence that is difficult to describe, but an experience that I can never forget. I had chosen a particular area in the wooded area as my praying ground. I had been praying, "Lord, have mercy on me, a sinner, and please save me."

I had prayed this continually, and after several days in earnest prayer, I had the experience that I related above about the Holy Spirit's presence. I ran to the house to tell my mother, but as I journeyed in to tell her, Satan said to me, "Now, you're going to go in and tell your mother that lie?" I turned around and went back to my praying ground. I questioned the Lord again because I thought I was going to have another experience that was more profound. The Lord impressed upon me, that "you've got all you're going to get." I then, went in to tell my mother of my conversion experience, and to this day, I do not remember physically leaving the wooded area going in to see my mother. It was as if I was caught up in the Spirit and transported from the wooded area to my mother's kitchen. My mother, of course, as any mother would, questioned me as to whether I was sure. I said yes. She was happy for me, and we agreed that I would make my open confession at the next church meeting.

Members of three generations got saved the night that I confessed Christ. I was the one of the young generation. The congregation and preacher were not particularly excited about my being saved. An old tough sinner and another grown-up had been saved and one of Fred's boys (that's me). The Lord had His hand on me. They might have thought it unimportant, but the Lord knew what He was doing. He was preparing me even then.

I was baptized in a pond. There were several of us baptized the same Sunday. The process was to place two sticks out into the pond on either side, and the preacher and a deacon would stand between them. They would call down the candidate, who was dressed in a white robe and white cap, and the preacher would lift his right hand and say, "In obedience to the Great Head of Heaven, I now baptize you in the name of the Father and of the Son and of the Holy Ghost." They then crossed your hands on your chest and submerged you totally under the water.

After that, we went back to church, redressed and took our first communion. The mothers of the church used muscadine grapes to make the wine.

The congregation wanted to make sure you knew how to pray. Once you were saved, you had to participate in prayer meeting the very next week. The deacons would call on you to pray. God had His hand on me.

Another thing that was taught was to pay your church dues (tithes). You must give to the Lord of your finances. That is why I say, to this day, methods may change, but the message is still the same. If there is no change in the mode, time will leave you behind. Change the method; do not change the message.

A strong emphasis was put on the new birth when I was growing up, and the mourner's benches were a part of the process. I have learned that they (mourner's benches) are not necessary in order to be saved. The Lord will save us the minute we believe and accept Him as our personal savior. This is an example of the method changing, but the message of salvation remains unchanged. You must be godly sorry for your sins and ask the Lord to forgive you. "You must be born again," says Jesus in *John 3:3.*

From the day of my conversion, I knew nothing could be the same. One of my favorite scriptures is *Romans 10:9, 10,* "If thou shalt confess with thy mouth the Lord Jesus and shalt believe in thine heart that God has raised Him up from the dead, thou shall be saved. For with the heart man believeth unto righteousness, with the mouth confession is made unto salvation."

The person reading this book may have some question as to why I was 13 years old when I was converted. Years ago, when I was a child, parents thought that the sins of the children were upon the parents until they were 13 years of age. This was just an old myth that people used because they said that Jesus was 12 years old when he went up into the temple. Because of this belief held by the church community at that time, I knew at age 13 that I needed a savior because I was no longer under the covering of my parents. I understood earlier and could have been saved earlier, but at that time, I believed in observing tradition so I waited until I was 13 years old. Thank God for his grace.

I enjoyed reading John 3:16 and 17 and many other wonderful scriptures. Shortly after my conversion Satan was on his job. (He speaks to us, too, you know.) When I first accepted Christ under that pine tree in the woods, and had the experience with Satan trying to place doubt in my mind about my experience, I learned one thing: When you reach a place of no return, meaning you are going to trust God no matter what, that's when the change comes. When I made up my mind that whether it was a lie or the truth, I was going to confess Christ as my Savior, that's when the work took place. As I stated earlier, I was under the pine tree and it was as if someone had a bucket of water (though it was not water) and poured it all over me. I was caught up in the Spirit and seemingly transported to my mother's kitchen. I do not remember leaving the tree coming to my mother's kitchen at all. Suddenly, I was in front of her telling her that I was saved and had received Christ as my personal Savior, i.e., "got religion."

After I made my confession to my mother, I attended the daytime revival meeting and walked down the aisle to make my confession to the congregation. As I told you, three generations were saved during that revival. Although I was called "Fred's boy," they did not know that the Lord had His hand on me and had destined me to become a preacher of the Gospel. That is why the scripture says, "For who hath despised the day of small things?" *(Zechariah 4:10)*.

As I stated above, my conversion experience was real. After I was converted there was a very noticeable change in my life. I think people should have a noticeable change because they are new creatures in Christ after the Holy Spirit is indwelling in them. The Holy Spirit is our guide. I will never forget my conversion experience. It was on a Tuesday morning, about 10:00 a.m.

The Holy Spirit kept me when I left home as a 16 year old teenager to go into the world of work to be on my own. I would come and go as I wanted because I worked and paid rent; however the Holy Spirit would not allow me to do those things that were not in line with Christian living. My landlady said she could set a clock by my footsteps in the evening, because she knew that I would come in at a decent hour. The Holy Spirit will also protect you. I would walk the streets and nothing happened to me physically. I was unafraid. I never encountered any trouble.

Even though my job was working on a beer truck, the Spirit did not allow me to fall into the temptation of getting drunk.

Because of His indwelling and my conversion, when I was in the military, many of the people that we met outside of the United States in Germany noted that there was something different about me. The Germans would say to me, "Why you no not act like the other soldiers?" I would place my hands in a prayerful gesture. They would ask "You be Christian?" and I would say, "Ja, Ja" (yah, yah). I was even asked by my company commander to conduct church services once when we were out in the woods during my tour in Germany. I told my superior officer that I was not a chaplain. He explained to me that he knew that, but that I could do it. I got my Bible and was ready to conduct the service, but the chaplain came. The Lord protects and keeps his hand on his own. Once you are converted you have a compass that keeps you from going too far out of bounds. That is a great blessing and one of the attributes of the indwelling of the Holy Spirit after you receive our Lord and Savior Jesus Christ. Jesus said he (the Holy Spirit) will guide us into truth *(John 16:13)*. Believers are sealed by the Holy Spirit.

Clarence W. Hopson - 18 years old

Fresh away from home; on my own and inexperienced with much to learn about life.

CHAPTER 3

TEEN YEARS AND CALL TO THE MINISTRY

"Remember now thy Creator in the days of thy youth,
while the evil days come not, nor the years draw nigh..."
Ecclesiastes 12:1a

As a fourteen year old teenager I had to handle the most difficult thing of my life–the death of my mother. I now understand that God had His hand on me, even then. In preparing for the ministry, I needed to know how to comfort the bereaved in the congregation He would have me shepherd later in life. For everything that a believer experiences, God has a purpose. *(Romans 8:28)*

When my mother passed late on a Saturday evening the first of January, 1943, nobody was there to comfort me. I was the only one of the boys at my mother's bedside when she died. I was standing there, and my mother asked me, "Where are the other children?" My dad was in town; my older brother had gone to get the doctor. For some reason, I had gone back to the house. The midwife was there. She was giving my mother smelling salt. My mother was tossing her head from side to side, saying, "Lord, I am turning my children over into your hand. Come and take me out of my misery." That had a great impact on me. My mother died in childbirth. The child she was giving birth to also died.

My grandmother started running through the woods yelling, "They have killed my daughter." There I was, the houseboy, very close to my mother and hearing my grandmother say these things instead of giving me and the other children some kind of comfort. She didn't mean to disregard our feelings of sadness at that time, but that had a very negative impact on me as a teen who had just lost his mother. It was also a learning experience for me, and that's why I talk to people during their time of loss.

After the funeral service, when you lose a loved one, the sadness really sets in. After the funeral is over and the quietness sets in because all of the company is gone, the ministry is sorely needed. That is a lonely time. In trying to cope with the loss of my mother, I tried to sleep it off. I grieved from January until April or May of 1943. I kept trying to sleep and sleep and sleep; I didn't like being awake. As long as I was awake, I was cognizant of the fact that my mother was no longer with us, but when I was sleeping she was alive.

The Lord has to break us and mold us for His work. I had no idea I was going to be a pastor and a counselor and have to help people overcome the loss of their loved ones, but the Lord knew. He was preparing me. One night my mother came to me in a vision. She and my aunt came to our house in a car, but the only person who got out was my mother. She asked me, "Who did your daddy marry?" I said, "He married Miss Willie Bell and she is real nice to us, but why don't you come back with us?" She said, "but I can't come back." She disappeared and that simple experience cured me. From that day to this I have had no problems dealing with death. The hand of the Lord was upon me. The Lord had not forgotten me, because I had accepted Him as my personal savior at that time. Even when my father died, I handled the funeral arrangements along with one of my brothers and comforted the rest of the family. The experience I had with my mother was a part of my preparation for the ministry. You can't tell a person what God can do until you have had some experiences yourself. God's Word is true and is there to guide you. That's why Romans 8:28 is so important. "And we know that all things work together for good to them that love God, to them who are the called according to his purpose." Whatever a Christian is experiencing he can be sure God has a purpose for it. We may not understand it, but God has a purpose for it. Nothing can happen to a believer outside the permissive will of God. That's why Paul said in Romans 5:3, "We glory in tribulations."

During this time World War II broke out, but I was too young to be drafted. None of my brothers served in the military during WWII. Later on, however, my brother and I did go to the Army and served during the Korean Conflict. My parents said that they prayed that we would not go. I don't know why. During the war, money became plentiful. My oldest brothers moved to Jackson and found employment. I followed them later.

I left home at age 16. I went to live with one of my brothers. I got my first job. I was a truck helper on a beer truck. We hauled, loaded and unloaded beer all over the city of Jackson, Mississippi, and other small towns in the vicinity. We also delivered to various hotels, restaurants, and tavern establishments.

When I left home, my brother and I paid my dad to let us move away from home. Times have really changed. It's hard to get this generation to leave home. Even though my job was hauling beer, I did not drink it because I was a Christian. I have been told that it is not unusual for a woman to have grown up and not indulge in drinking, but highly unusual for a young man—well, I am one of those rare men, so I know it is possible. I tasted it, and I disliked the flavor. I have never been drunk in my life. I have never been high, even though I was out in the world living on my own with no one to tell me when and where to go. I know when a person is born again he has the guidance of the Holy Spirit.

I had my calling of the Lord to preach when I was about 17 or 18 years of age. I know the hand of the Lord was upon me. I read the whole book of the Revelation. It was the first book of the Bible that I had ever read. All of it fascinated me. I didn't know the word 'whore' was in the Bible. I read it with enthusiasm. While reading Revelation, I had a vision. When you dream, you forget; when you have a vision, you remember. I saw the whole world disappear—people were running everywhere—the whole world was caving in. I was standing on this place in the world and the person who was standing behind me was someone I'd never seen. The whole world disappeared except where we were standing. When I attempted to run, this person grabbed me on the shoulder and said to me, "This will not cave in." This was my first calling. I said to the Lord, "If you want me to preach, let me get a good wife."

You have to be careful what you ask God for. He will give you what you ask for. My wife and I have never been apart in the more than 49 years of marriage except when our daughter was sick. I told the Lord to let me get a good wife and I would preach. Well, I forgot my promise. My friend and I ran all over Mississippi dating girls and having the time of our life, so we thought. The Lord did not forget. After my stint in the military, after my marriage, and after my move to Chicago, God reminded me of that calling and got my attention again.

Five years after my wife and I were married, the Lord began to whip me and make me aware of my promises. I was working in Melrose Park at the International Harvester plant. (That's why I am living in the suburbs of Chicago today.) I carpooled with four men that also worked at the plant, and sometimes I would get so sick my wife would have to come to the plant to get me. I would go to the doctor, and he could find nothing wrong. We would have company over for the evening, and I could not entertain them. I would just get sick and have to leave the living room and go into the bedroom to lie down. The doctor still could find nothing wrong.

Once when I was laid off from Harvester and my dad was ill, I went to visit him. We talked all night. He told me that he had been called to preach and did not go. He said, "Hank (that's my nickname), now you are going to have to preach. God is going to bring preaching out in my children, and I'm going to get out of the way so you can raise my grandchildren."

God is really a person who relates to his creation. I promised Him I would preach. I was at work on the line and just preaching my heart out. God works with our minds and thoughts. When I would come home from work my family would be in bed asleep. I went to the bathroom and sat down. (People say this is not a good place to be called, but for me it was.) I had heard a preacher in Mississippi say that because he was disobedient to God's call, God took his whole family before he would accept his calling. I did not want the Lord to take my family. I said to Him, "I am tired of running. Lord, if you want me to preach, let me know." In my mind, the Lord said to me, "You trust me for salvation; now trust me to preach." I needed a second sign from the Lord.

I was very active in the church. I was the youngest deacon on the Deacon Board and also a Sunday School teacher. I was working the second shift at Harvester in Melrose Park and would get off at midnight; the Lord told me to read Titus–Chapter 1, Verse 5. This was my confirmation. It reads

"For this cause left I thee in Crete, that thou shouldest set in order the things that are wanting, and ordain elders in every city, as I had appointed thee." I told my wife that I had been called to preach the Gospel of Jesus Christ. She said, "You are going to tell the folks that?" I said, "Yes." I told my pastor that I had been called to preach.

The pastor arranged for me to preach what is known in the Baptist church as one's trial sermon. When the time arrived, the house was full because I was well known. My oldest brother who was pastoring a small church at the time in Chicago came to support me. The Holy Spirit was upon me and I was able to deliver the sermon very well.

I am noting this next experience for other young preachers. *I* decided to preach at my brother's church that following Sunday from Matthew 25, "The five wise and five foolish virgins." Remember, *I* was going to preach it. I didn't ask God anything. Many of our relatives and friends came to hear me. I was flat as I could be. If I could have crawled out of the backdoor I would have. The Lord taught me that I couldn't preach apart from Him. From that day to now, I never attempt to preach without asking God, "Lord what do you want me to say to your people?" I learned quickly that I can't preach of myself. Since these two experiences, I have been preaching, and the Lord has blessed.

PFC. Clarence W. Hopson in basic training at Camp Gordon, Georgia - early 1950s.

PFC. Hopson on training exercise at Fort Bragg Camp, North Carolina-early 1950s.

CHAPTER 4

MILITARY SERVICE

"And hath redeemed us from our enemies;
for his mercy endureth forever."
Psalm 136:24

I left home at age 16 during WWII. I was glad to be on my own working and being responsible for myself. I never lost my commitment to Christ. Something (the Holy Spirit ministering within) told me what to do. I went to prayer meeting on Wednesdays, read my Bible through and meditated on God's word. I was the only young person in prayer meeting. I had a real thirst for God's word. The Lord had His hand on me.

In 1950 the Church gave me a Bible and took up an offering for me when I was drafted into the Army. I treasured their gifts and was grateful. Even though I was not a preacher, my pastor stopped in the middle of the revival and raised an offering for me. This pastor also married my wife and me when I was discharged from the Army.

I was 22 years old when I went into Military Service. I was inducted into the U. S. Army in Jackson, Mississippi. We had to go to Arkansas for our physical and rationing of new Army uniforms. I was assigned to the Army's Signal Corps at Camp Gordon, Georgia. They called me the preacher. When we first arrived at Camp Gordon, Georgia, from Camp Chaffee, Arkansas, to do our basic training, I had missed church services for several Sundays and was hungry for the Word. Because we had not been there long enough to get passes, I decided to preach myself. The other soldiers who heard me preaching in the shower after we got to the camp would be looking over each other's shoulders trying to see who was preaching in the shower. I was preaching my heart out. Even the sergeant called me "Rev." That is how I got the title of "Rev." We were shipped over seas to Germany in service of our country. While in Stuttgart,

Germany, one time the sergeant asked me to speak to the troops. I told him that I was not a preacher, and he said, "I know that, but you know what to tell them." The Lord had His hand on me and was preparing me to be his preacher. I prepared my message and we had an overflow crowd of soldiers in the chapel, but the Army chaplain did arrive in time to preach. The soldiers were disappointed because they wanted to hear me.

I spent two years in the Army. When our ship left Germany, a mighty storm arose, and I had to stand guard one night; the storm was so active that the ship was leaning almost horizontal. I remember singing Mahalia Jackson's song, "He Rides The Raging Sea, Yes He Does, Yes He Does." That storm lasted for five days. I was not afraid even though my guard post was on the lower side of the ship. During the voyage home, one of the security personnel threw a rescue torch into the sea. As far as I could see, whenever the torch was on the top of the wave, I could see the glow from the light. My post was on the lower side of the ship, so I could direct the soldiers to the upper side of the deck in order to give some balance. It took us 10 days coming back. The last five days were beautiful. We landed in New York Harbor in October of 1952. When we landed in New York the sea was calm. The Statue of Liberty was there welcoming us and looking good. It was one of the most beautiful days I had ever seen. We were back at home at last. It is a good feeling for a citizen to have served his country well and then be welcomed back after a job well done. Military service teaches one discipline and self-control. I think this is a good experience for every young man.

Before I went into military service, I worked at McRae's Department Store in Jackson, where I stamped price tags in new clothes. While there, a young white female clerk who was overly friendly befriended me. The Lord protected me, even then. I could have gotten in trouble because of her actions being misinterpreted at that time in history. Remember, segregation was still very much alive. The Lord had His hand on me.

Wedding Day of Clarence W. Hopson and Annie Bell Drakes
at New Hope Baptist Church in Jackson, Mississippi, January 18, 1953

CHAPTER 5

MARRIAGE, MOVE AND CONTINUED EDUCATION

"Whoso findeth a wife findeth a good thing, and obtaineth favour of the Lord."
Proverbs 18:22

My wife's maiden name was Annie Bell Drakes. Her parents were Foster and Comfort Drakes of Jackson, Mississippi. Her father was a heavy equipment operator, where he operated the large caterpillars and bulldozers across the states of Mississippi, Arkansas and Louisiana, building highways and roadways. Her mother was a pastry cook at the Edward Hotel in Jackson. She was an excellent cook of all kinds of sweet treats. The first time I saw my wife I was about 18 or 19 years old. She came to visit her aunt. I found her attractive, dignified and very wholesome. She wore glasses and looked very studious. She stayed with her aunt and attended Lanier High School. I was a paying roomer at this home. As a young man I called her my "play sister." She refused to date me because she had a rule that she would not date a man who lived in the same building with her. Because this was her rule, I complied. I did, however, occasionally take her to the movies–as her brother.

After I left Jackson and went into the Army, I would write Annie and my two sisters letters. They were my biological sisters and she was my "play sister." One day when I was home on leave and was taking her to the movies, I told her, "I'm tired of this sister stuff; I want to be your boyfriend." She agreed. When I went back to the camp, I wrote her a letter different from the ones to my biological sisters, this time. I started the letter with "Dearest Darling." When I went overseas, I would get leaves from the trees and scented paper and write her about what it was like at the various locations. I thought I was romantic. Of course, she wrote me back. I remember writing her and saying I would ask for her hand in marriage if she had not found someone else.

Before I went overseas she came to Atlanta to go to Nightingale Nursing School. I was stationed in Augusta, Georgia, and I went to see her. She roomed with a Mr. and Mrs. Taylor. A male friend of hers sent her a bouquet of flowers every week; he was studying to be a doctor. She wasn't getting anything from me but letters. Apparently, the letters meant more to her than the flowers. When I came home for Christmas, I proposed marriage and she accepted. Our courtship was very short. When I came home we had a few dates. I said we would get married if she wanted to. Her friend, this medical student, sent her a set of rings. She let me see them and asked me, "What am I to do?" I told her to send them back to him.

My pastor's wife, Mrs. Pickens, helped us arrange our marriage ceremony since I was a member of that congregation. I was as green as grass. I knew nothing about preparing for a formal wedding. The Lord's hand was upon me.

I remember that during the time of the wedding preparations, when my wife and I were getting ready, we had a little argument and I thought she was going to say, well, I don't want to marry you. She doesn't know this, but I was getting scared. But the day of the marriage, when the music stopped, with the wedding party in place and a quietness fell over the room. I took her by the hand. I had just gotten out of the Army...I was a strong young man and thought I knew how to handle it. When the hush fell over the church and finally the preacher said, "Dearly Beloved, we are gathered here to..." I actually passed out. I didn't fall on the floor, but in my mind I really passed out. For a few seconds, I went completely blind. I mean I couldn't see anything. If someone had asked me my name, I could not have told them. I guess as men, we feel we are losing our freedom. I don't know what it is, but I learned two things about that. One is that marriage is sacred. The other is that the marriage ceremony brings with it the realization that you are stepping into another stage of life. It is a different ball game when you are going to be responsible for a wife and be the head of a household. Maybe this is why so many men are reluctant to get married.

Remember, I asked the Lord to give me a good wife. He did. At this writing, my wife and I have been married for more than 49 years. God keeps his promise.

It is wrong for ministers or any person to counsel young people that they will not have conflicts when they marry. My wife and I had our spats as a young couple and still do from time to time. Personalities clash. This experience of living a married life has been invaluable in my counseling sessions with young prospective brides and grooms. My wife and I both have very strong personalities. We both want to get our points across. The beauty of marriage is to reconcile after disagreements. Besides, making up is fun.

My wife and I got married January 18, 1953, and relocated to Chicago a few months later. We were newlyweds who came to Chicago seeking better employment opportunities because we wanted to start our family. And, of course, I found employment at International Harvester in Melrose Park, Illinois. I was living in Chicago and housing was very difficult to find. The Korean War was going on and these were difficult times. I moved to Chicago a month ahead of my wife. She told me to find a place for us to stay because she was coming to join me in Chicago. I got a place. We had one room. We had to share bathroom facilities with other families in the building. This was hard for both of us. It was not like the large homes we had both left in Mississippi.

I was excited. I had found a good job. My wife was now joining me in our first new home. I went to the train station, picked up my wife and brought her to our first home, the one room, which I had freshly painted. I'd bought new linens and pillows and had it spit-shine clean. My wife starting crying. I told her, "If you are going to be a baby, you should have stayed home with your momma." This is tough. We struggled and went on from there.

My wife does not allow the church to dictate to her anything about her taste in clothing, jewelry, etc. She let me know that she likes to dress the way she wants to dress. She likes fashionable clothes, and she wears them well.

I am a Pauline preacher, in that I made a vow that I would never own a Cadillac or have an Anniversary, because it could cause someone to stumble. Since I was not a seminary preacher, I had the experience of learning what the rank and file had to say about preachers and their conduct. One of the main excuses some people give for not coming to the church is that the conduct of the preachers leaves a lot to be desired, especially in the area of the kind of cars they drive. (We know, however, that is not a valid reason.) They also feel that all the preachers want are big cars and a lot of women. Even though this is a misconception, in most cases, I promised that I would not be engaged in any conduct that would be a stumbling block to any person accepting Christ as his or her personal savior. This has been a bone of contention in my household because my wife feels she has the right to drive whatever she wants to drive, and she does. I drive either a Mercury or a mini-van. They get me where I want to go. They are fully equipped and have everything on them that the luxury cars have. I have been told by many men that they have been encouraged to make a commitment to the Lord because of my conduct in this area.

When the church was smaller, my wife was the Training Union director for a period of time and she was also the general program chairperson. My oldest brother who was pastoring in Denver counseled her in the role of the pastor's wife. He specifically told her that she should not be present at the business meetings because sometimes things might get heated and she, of course, would not take kindly to that with reference to her husband, even though he is the pastor. She aids me a lot in that she knows nearly as many people by name as I do. If a member is missing for a few Sundays, she will let me know and remind me that maybe I should check on them. When members ask her about her job, she lets them know that her job is to aid me and to take care of me. I have been encouraging her to teach, and she tells me that everyone does not have the gift of teaching, even though she had training at Moody Bible Institute. She is active in our hospitality ministry.

After I was discharged from the Army, married and moved to Chicago, I decided to go back to school under the GI bill. I attended and graduated from Crane High School, as an adult. Then, I went to Wells Evening School where I took courses in psychology, public speaking, typing and business law. Every pastor needs to take a course in business law. You need to be comfortable when you are in a legal setting. Pastors need to know this in order to be good administrators. The secular psychology I took at Wells was a great help to me. When I went to Moody, of course, I took Christian psychology. Both courses are invaluable in the ministerial duties that I must perform for the cause of Christ. I also took a course at Coyne Electrical School for television repair.

I went to Moody part-time until I graduated on May 11, 1971. I was determined; I went sick or well. I took an interesting, difficult and required course at Moody called Bible Geography. It was particularly difficult because we had to draw maps and memorize and spell those hard biblical names. I once challenged my teacher, Dr. Gardner, who was from Memphis. I said, "Dr. Gardner, do you expect us to put in all those hard words and do all those things?" He looked me right in the eye and said, "Brother Hopson, I tell you something, I learned one thing a long time ago, if you don't expect too much from people, you're not going to get too much out of them. You can do it, and I expect you to do it." I tucked my head and went out. He really set the pace for my studying. Even though I got 50 on the first exam, I ended up with a B+ on the final exam, and of course, I passed the course.

I had trouble with one other subject and that was Music Appreciation. It was the only course I failed at Moody. An older retired gentleman from Bell Telephone Company and I were the most inept students in that class. I thought singing was the only class requirement. Well, I was very misinformed. We were expected to write and transpose music. The next semester I took Music Theory and, with the coaching of Mrs. Shine, the instructor, I finally passed with a C. I had to have Music in order to graduate from Moody. I took it in my junior year because I knew I would not pass it the first time. I did not want to wait until my senior year to take a course, fail and not be able to graduate.

I was asked which curriculum I wanted to follow. I told them the pastor's curriculum. I did not want to be a chaplain or a prison chaplain. I did not want my children to be raised in that environment. Moody puts its graduates in contact with various churches that are looking for pastors or chaplains to fill the various available positions. I was offered many preaching engagements from different parts of the country, some from as far away as Bronx, New York, and Seattle, Washington. I only responded to the churches in the Chicago vicinity. I preached at a Church in Milwaukee and Kankakee. In fact, my first preaching engagement after graduation from Moody was at New Morning Star in Kankakee, Illinois.

However, I knew the Lord did not want me there. He had his hand on me for another assignment.

When I was in school, it was very difficult for me to follow a script because I just don't like preaching from a script. I like to preach straight from the heart as the Lord gives it to me. When I was at Moody, I was already preaching. Sometimes, after I would finish my sermons, the teacher would say to the class, "Didn't that really touch your heart?" I graduated from Moody on May 11, 1971, and Broadview Baptist called me in May of 1972.

I like *Zechariah 4:10a:* "For who hath despised the day of small things? For they shall rejoice...." God knew he wanted me at Broadview, even though it was very small and basically unstructured. This would give God the opportunity to use me for the structuring of the Church the way he wanted it. If I had gone to an established church, it would have taken me six to eight years to tear down many of their old ingrained traditions. I'm often asked why the Church is growing by leaps and bounds. I explain that it is easier to lead young people who do not have the baggage of tradition weighing them down. When we follow scripture, God will give the increase.

Rev. Clarence W. Hopson at home with his oldest children, Priscilla, Denise and Wilbur during the early years as new and proud father - Chicago, Illinois apartment.

CHAPTER 6

CHILDREN ARE A BLESSING

"Lo, children are an heritage of the Lord..."
Psalm 127a

Although I met my wife in my late teens, we married when I was 24 years old. An older man, who was my Sunday School superintendent, once told me that if you didn't marry by the time you were 25 years old, chances are you would not. Of course, those were different times than now. The old folks thought that if you waited too long, you would be too set in your own ways and too selfish to want to share your life with someone else forever, i.e., you would have seen too much in other relationships.

I am the father of five children, Priscilla Ann Hopson Craig, Wilbur Hopson, Comfort Denise Hopson Brown, LaVerne Hopson and Jeffrey Hopson.

My wife and children have been a real joy in my life. I like married life, and I love children. As each one of my children reached adulthood, they remembered the good times we had as a family during their childhood years. My family life is truly a blessing of the Lord.

My oldest daughter, of course, was the first to leave home and go off to college. The other two daughters followed her later. I had a family custom that I practiced whenever one of the girls was going away to college, "fatherly advice for the college bound girl." I'd have this little talk after the family had gone out to dinner and had a good time. I have also shared this information with members of the church who go off to college: "In college there are leaders and followers; you have to decide whether you are going to be a leader or a follower. But one thing I want you to remember, whatever you do, make sure it is something you want to do. Don't let someone else influence you into doing something by a dare. For sure, you will encounter these kinds of people in colleges. I want you to know that whatever you do, you make sure you are doing it because you want to do it. If you do something that is not right, do not jump out of a window and kill yourself. We still love you. If you get pregnant, we still love you. So don't you panic, thinking "Daddy doesn't love me" or "Mom is disappointed in me." We still love you, and we will try to work through this. I have said this to every one of my children and many other church members' children, especially during the time of the year when we give our church scholarships for our students who are leaving their homes for the first time to go away to college.

Now, back to my oldest daughter, Priscilla. She later married, of course, and has a son, our first grandson. That was really a thrill. You really learn to appreciate *Proverbs 17:6*: "Children's children are the crown of old men; and the glory of children are their fathers." Our oldest son, Wilbur, entered the working world when he reached adulthood. Our next daughter, Denise, went away to college, got married and now has three children, one of whom is currently in college. It is a blessing to live to see your grandchildren in college. Our third daughter, LaVerne, went away to college and is a career woman in one the major metropolitan cities in our country. Our youngest son, Jeffrey, married and has one son. That is my youngest grandson, and the only one that we are able to see on a regular basis. All of our children accepted Christ as their personal savior when they were young, and for that I am eternally grateful.

Now, my wife and I can go visit them in the various cities where they reside and see the fruit of our labor. I had always taught them that when they grew up I wanted them to move away from home and reside in another city so we would have somewhere to go. Now, sometimes I wonder whether or not they got too far away, because we have to go such a long way to visit. We find that we don't get a chance to see our grandchildren as often as we would like to because of the distance.

I give my wife a lot of credit for rearing the children. Many times I would be busy with church activities, classes in college or evening school, and a lot of the child rearing fell on her. I am appreciative of her dedication to the children and me. My wife was a very firm mother and in these days, that is a good quality in order to rear children. Tough love is alive and well. This experience as a husband and father has been both enjoyable and very helpful to me in the ministry. Since my wife and I have raised five children I can counsel persons in marriage and child rearing. People cannot tell me what can and cannot be done in rearing children. This experience, too, was helpful to me in the ministry, especially in the area of family counseling. The Lord truly laid his hand on me.

CHAPTER 7

WORK AT PILGRIM REST BAPTIST CHURCH IN CHICAGO

"Study to shew thyself approved unto God, a workman that needeth not to be ashamed, rightly dividing the word of truth."
2 Timothy 2:15

After being called to preach by the Lord, and being unable to rest or stay physically well because of my not acknowledging my calling, I finally told my pastor. I said to Rev. Matthew Thomas, pastor of Pilgrim Rest Baptist Church, 1901 W. Washington Blvd., Chicago, Illinois, that the Lord had indeed called me to be a preacher of the Gospel of Jesus Christ.

I was already actively teaching in the Sunday School Department. I had one of the largest classes in the Sunday School. I was, however, called to preach not to teach Sunday School. We must remember that no matter how noble our work for the Lord, we must follow our calling. Teaching Sunday School was not my calling. This applies to anyone who has had a call on their life to be in a particular vineyard of the Lord's work. Be sure to be obedient to your own calling. We, however, often try to work around what God tells us to do. When we do this, we are not in God's will. We must be obedient.

The pastor set a date for me to preach my trial sermon. My trial sermon was preached on a Wednesday night. The house was packed with people who had come to hear me preach. The church capacity was about 500 persons. My brothers and many other family members came to hear my trial sermon.

The Lord gave me the message for the night. I will never forget it. The text came from Matthew 22:42. My sermon was "What Think ye of Christ, Whose Son is He?" I used for a theme, "Your Opinion of Christ." The message was well received.

As I mentioned in Chapter 3, one of my brothers who was the pastor of the King David Missionary Baptist Church in Chicago asked me to come over and preach for him. The Lord taught me a very important lesson. I, of course, agreed to go right away. I didn't ask God for a message for that Sunday.

Since this is so important for young ministers to remember, please allow me to reiterate the story. At King David Church, even more of my relatives came to hear me preach. That Sunday morning, my sermon was "The Ten Virgins; Five Wise and Five Foolish." I fell flat on my face. I could have crawled out the back door. This was one of the greatest lessons I would ever learn. Every young preacher should learn that he should consult God before he preaches. He should ask God what He wants him to say. I have learned to say, "God, this is your message. These are your people. Now you tell me what You want me to tell them." God showed me I cannot preach without conferring with Him. I had to learn that without Him, I can do nothing. From that day to this I have never again gotten up before God's people to preach without asking God what He wanted me to say. He has never failed me yet. I was an evangelist for 15 years and have been a pastor for 30 years. I always ask the Lord what he wants me to say to his people. I am God's messenger. I have preached all over Chicago and the State of Illinois, but not without consulting God first.

I am proud of my 15 years of evangelizing; it was truly a learning experience for me. I have seen the good and the not so good. I've preached in large, medium and small churches. During my years of evangelistic work, I've also preached in storefront churches. I profited from some of the errors that I saw pastors make. It doesn't mean I haven't made any errors; it just means that I have not made as many. Being observant taught me to recognize acceptable boundaries. I learned from their mistakes. Truly, the Lord had His hand on me.

When I preach, my desire is that men might be saved. Our present church is an evangelistic church. That has always been my thrust. When my wife and I joined Pilgrim Rest, we did not have any children. We were there for 10 years. We started our family while we were members of that church. We had always been used to seeing the church open on Sunday nights.

The devil is busy at night and here the Church doors are closed. That, I think, is a problem, today. I think Churches should be open at night. Pilgrim Rest was near Chicago Stadium, and there were constant interruptions from the stadium activities. We had parking problems at night. I was the new kid on the block in my Sunday School class. We had a young minister who was our Sunday School teacher. I would point out to him when something was not in sync with the scripture. I would always show it to him in the Bible. He was receptive. I was not trying to take over his job, but when there is a discrepancy, the Word of God can clarify it. Even though I was a layman, my knowledge of the scripture and adherence was keen, and it caused me to rise to the top, as it were. God had blessed me with a good understanding, and I did share. When my wife and I first went to Pilgrim Rest we had no car. Some of the members were kind to us and would pick us up and drive us home.

At Pilgrim Rest we developed the Sunday School into three departments, the adult department, youth department and children's department. We had a parent who could not part with her children to go to the children's department. She insisted that her children stay with her in the adult department. In this case, her children may as well have stayed home because they did not understand what the adults were talking about. Sometimes it is difficult to make some parents understand. This may be a simple thing to us, but to them it is a real issue. In such cases we must seek God's guidance and hope the person comes to an understanding of how children develop. Just as they are grouped in public school, the children need to be with their peers in Sunday School.

Later, they asked me to teach the young adult class. I was always against selling dinners in the church, which was an old fundraising custom in African American Baptist churches. The fact of the matter is the congregation should have been tithing, which, of course, eliminates the necessity of this antiquated practice. They said I was ruining the young adults.

They had a men's class and a woman's class. They gave me the adult women. After studying scripture, the women said they would not go into the kitchen to cook anymore. Then, they gave me the men's class. Each class felt convicted by the Word and was against cooking and selling dinners. They started to call them the Hopson Bunch. I was called a rabble-rouser. I was not an agitator, but whenever you point out evil you make people uncomfortable. However, I did not worry, because the hand of the Lord was upon me.

Next I was given the teenagers, ages 12 to 14, whom I taught until we moved our membership. I taught these teens for 3 or 4 years. I gave them homework. My best asset is teaching. I taught those young people well. When I first took the class, it was chaotic. Learning was nil. The first thing I had to do was to get some order and institute some discipline. Some of the children said I was too tough, but others responded positively. The leadership of the church left me alone after they gave me the teenagers. I taught my students with love.

When my family would take vacations, we visited the homes of some of the students to meet their parents, particularly, the students who had parents that did not attend church. The kids would get excited about their Sunday School teacher coming to see them. I learned that children love discipline, whether they say they do or not. They listen and obey when you show them love, caring and attention.

When we moved to Maywood, my class was invited to our new home and we would have 40 children eating hotdogs in our backyard. The Sunday School Superintendent had to split my class right down the middle because of its size; I had 17 kids and another teacher took 17. In less than three months, I was back up to 37 students. I made them do their homework each week. They had to bring me written reports of the assignments. I believe Sunday School should be as efficient as public school.

Four of our children were born during our time at Pilgrim Rest. My oldest daughter and son were ushers. I was on the deacon board until my call to the ministry. I wasn't afraid even though I was the youngest deacon on the board. Rev. Thomas gave me a lot of freedom. After I was called to preach, he made me Jr. Pastor. I preached every fifth Sunday. The church would be packed in the main auditorium and the balcony. There were people in attendance both for me and against me. Those who were for me came to support me and those who were against me didn't want to miss what I was going to say. God was raising me up and preparing me for pastoring. I didn't know that then. Pastor Thomas was always good to me and gave me a lot of freedom because he knew I was right according to scripture in both word and deed. I always respected his leadership.

My young people's class grew so fast that I kept moving from room to room. I went to the superintendent and told him my room was too small. The superintendent switched my classroom with a female teacher whose class was smaller. She went in and told the pastor that I had taken her room. Wisdom is being able to observe a given situation and deal righteously with it. The pastor came and asked me, "Who will you obey, me or the superintendent?" I told him I would go where they sent me. I refused to take sides. Finally, they gave me the room. These things will happen. God was raising me up to be a leader. A leader has to be strong and also face some hardships. As a leader, you must know how to mediate. All these things were learning experiences that would aid me in pastoring, not because I was so strong, but because the hand of the Lord was upon me.

The Lord put me in the inner city of Chicago like He did the children of Israel when he put them in Babylon so that I could get a belly full of idolatry, i.e., anniversaries and birthdays, etc. This is another antiquated practice in some churches where the birthdays and anniversaries of the pastor and various others are given a special day of celebration. I will address this in more detail later in the book. God sent me to preach in various inner city churches so I could get my fill of preachers taking advantage of the people. I saw preachers habitually fleecing the congregations. This is not true of all inner city pastors, but true of many I encountered. I said then, if I ever became a pastor, I would never have an anniversary or a birthday celebration in the church. To this day, 30 years later, I have never had one. I believe the House of the Lord is where we worship God and not man!!

We left Pilgrim Rest Baptist Church after 10 years of service. One day my wife and I were coming home and I told my wife that the Lord had spoken to me. The Lord said we ought to move our membership. I use my wife for confirmation when the Lord has spoken to me. My wife agreed. I went to the pastor and told him. We left in January of 1964. When I left they wanted to know what the young people were going to do without Rev. Hopson. The Lord had spoken and we moved our membership to First Baptist Church in Melrose Park. I wasn't worried about the young people at Pilgrim Rest because I knew the Lord was in control and he always has someone to carry on his program. As always, the hand of the Lord was guiding me.

CHAPTER 8

MOVE TO WESTERN SUBURBS

"...Go ye into all the world, and preach the gospel to every creature."
Mark 16:15b

In January of 1964 we moved our membership from Pilgrim Rest Baptist Church in Chicago to First Baptist Church in Melrose Park, Illinois. I believe in doing things in an orderly manner. We were starting a new year, and I felt that we should start the new year out in our new church home. By then, I had bought my first house in Illinois, and it was in Maywood, a suburb adjacent to Melrose Park. I was also working in the suburbs, and this would complete the move. Now, my home, my job and my church were all in Chicago's western suburbs. Besides, the most important issue had been settled; the Lord had spoken to me and told me it was time to move.

We received our letter from Pilgrim Rest Baptist Church and presented it to the First Baptist Church. I always feel that a practicing Christian should move from fellowship to fellowship by letter and not Christian experience. There is nothing wrong with moving by Christian experience, but sometimes it gives the impression that you have been inactive for a long time. If this is the case, then, of course, it is acceptable. Christians, however, who are current and actively participating in a fellowship should get a letter, if at all possible.

When I first came to the Melrose Park church family, it was a small church, which had a membership of approximately 150 members. The Pastor, Reverend Harry McNelty, told me he was going to build a new church. He spoke with a lot of faith. Even though I was the "new kid on the block," I threw myself into witnessing in the community. The church began to grow. I was glad that he allowed me to be a part of the new church negotiations, because even though I did not know it at the time, the Lord was preparing me for the next level of leadership in His vineyard. I was active in the Sunday School, acted as the pastor's assistant and worked on the building committee.

I have always felt that the teaching ministry is crucial to any church's growth. The members need to know what "thus says the Lord," and the only way they are going to know His word is to study, study, study. I worked long and hard with the Sunday School department. Sometimes I was perceived as being pushy, but here again, I just wanted to get the job done for the Lord and in an appropriate manner. We had changes in some key positions in the Sunday School department; then the Sunday School began to grow.

Because I believed so strongly in Christian education, I was made head of the Christian Education department. We gave gifts of encouragement to our students. Many have gone out into the secular world as true witnesses for the Lord and have told me that it was because of the training they received in the Christian Education department at the First Baptist Church in Melrose Park.

With the various departments running in an orderly manner, we began to make preparations for the acquisition of the new church. We were growing by leaps and bounds. At that time, few African-Americans had land in Melrose Park. Next to our church were two empty lots for sale. However, the owner did not want to sell them to us because we were Black. We went into prayer that the Lord would open his heart and have him sell them to us. He was asking an exorbitant price for them. This, of course, was to discourage us from trying to buy them. Another minister and I prayed while Rev. McNelty called the owner of the property. We were unaware that the owner was ill at the time. He sold the property for a fraction of the cost that he had previously asked. Our prayers had been answered.

Many times in life the Lord makes us an understudy so we can learn something about an area in which we have no expertise. I feel I was put on the building committee for that very purpose. Who, except God, would know that I would be in the midst of a building project many years down the road. He is truly awesome. This experience helped me both in the renovation of Broadview's first and second home as well as the acquisition of our third home. Much more goes into building a church than meets the eye. Many problems arise in building a new church that cause much stress on the leadership.

I did a lot of preaching at First Baptist in Melrose Park because my pastor was still in seminary. I presided over the Wednesday night prayer meeting. Pastor McNelty, who was my pastor until his recent death, gave me a lot of freedom in performing duties in the church. The Lord was priming me for pastoring then, even though I did not know it.

I never sought to be a pastor. I would never ask for that job. I served at First Baptist for eight years as Rev. McNelty's right hand. I was never officially named the assistant pastor. I knew my role was to undergird whatever my pastor said. I never disagreed with him, and if I did, the parishioners did not know it. An associate minister must be careful not to cause division in the church.

When Rev. McNelty's anniversary came each year, I worked as hard as everyone else. I worked hard to raise as much money as I could for him. I worked 100% for his program. This was his program. I was there to support him, although personally, I did not believe in pastor's anniversary celebrations.

After graduating from Moody Bible Institute in 1971, I was offered a lot of invitations to preach to various congregations across the Chicagoland area. One church, the Berean Baptist Church of Milwaukee, Wisconsin, called me to preach for them. This was the first church that started to call me "pastor." This was an integrated church. My wife and children did not like the city of Milwaukee. I told them that if that was where the Lord wanted me to go, we'd just have to go, because we were going to obey the Lord. Of course, when the church called me, they found out that they were not large enough to support my family. This church was in a convention in Ohio, and one of the gentlemen from the convention called me up and said that the people loved me in Milwaukee. He said the convention would give me a salary supplement of $250 per month. That was a very hard decision for me to make. But, of course, the Lord was in control, and he began to magnify my workload in the Chicagoland area, particularly in the stewardship area.

I remembered a preacher in Mississippi saying that the Lord had to take half of his family before he became obedient. I prayed to the Lord to give me the proper direction since I did not want to lose any of my family because I was in disobedience. When my workload became so overwhelming in the Chicagoland area, I felt that the Lord was telling me that this was where my field of labor was to be. I wrote a letter to the gentleman from the convention in Ohio letting them know of my decision. He asked me if I was sure, and I told him I was as sure of that as I was of my conversion. He called me up and thanked me for my honesty.

First Baptist built a beautiful new edifice for the Lord. During all of this time when I was preaching at various churches across the Chicagoland area, I was still a member at First Baptist. One day, I told my wife that my work at First Baptist was finished. I knew it was finished. The spirit had left me for working there. I was just marking time. I knew my work was done at that local assembly. The Lord knew that he was going to be sending me to a new vineyard.

CHAPTER 9

CALL TO FIRST PASTORATE AT BROADVIEW BAPTIST CHURCH

"And I will give you pastors according to mine heart,
which shall feed you with knowledge and understanding."
Jeremiah 3:15

It is critically important to follow the leading of the Holy Spirit in making decisions. I want to emphasize this to the new preachers or divinity students who may be reading this book. Secular knowledge and planning is good, but the leading of the Holy Spirit is superior to our knowledge and all of our plans.

At the time that Broadview Baptist was offering me the position of Pastor, I had been a guest preacher at a well-developed church on the south side of Chicago in a very lovely neighborhood. The church was located at 90th and Merrill Avenue. It was fully paid for and had a retiring pastor. The pastor was German and the congregation had me over to preach for them two or three times.

A week before I was called to Broadview, my family and I had dinner in the home of the pastor of the Merrill Avenue church, where he informed me that the congregation really liked me. He wanted me to consider taking over the pastorate, if it was the Lord's will. I thanked him, I could have yielded to the temptation to accept the pastorate of the Merrill Avenue church because it seemed a more fertile ground, but not only had I been counseled to go where the Lord was leading me by the gentleman from Ohio, as I mentioned before, and by this pastor, but also I was convicted in my own heart that I was God's servant and I was determined to follow the lead of the Holy Spirit. It was not to Merrill Avenue, but to an undeveloped church in the western suburbs, namely Broadview. I had preached at Broadview Baptist Chapel (as it was called at that time, because it had not been fully constituted as a church) and they called me to be their pastor. The very next week the church on Merrill Avenue called me. But, remember, God wants you to be where He wants you to be. The contrast was very glaring. One church was attractive, paid for, and had a pastor who was retiring. The other church was a small mission, not even a constituted church, with fewer than 40 members, where 80% of them were children, and it didn't even have a permanent building for worship.

Even though I had accepted Broadview, I could have changed my decision. This is where it is important to listen to the Spirit, no matter how glaring the contrasts. Remember, the pastor at Merrill Avenue and the gentleman in Ohio both offered to make it very comfortable and convenient for me financially. I thanked the Merrill Avenue pastor and told him that I had accepted the call to pastor the Broadview Baptist Chapel.

On the First Sunday in May 1972, I became the pastor of Broadview Baptist Chapel. I was called to my first pastorate at age 44. It had a church membership of about 40 people. We keep that list in our library as part of our history. When I came to Broadview they had $900.00 in their savings account and $800.00 in their checking account. I got this information from Brother William Rorer, who was the only man they had. We had no physical facilities. We held services in the Chicago Metropolitan Baptist Association building. We only had a desk and a chair that was given to us by the sponsoring church, Northwestern Baptist Church. They sponsored us as a mission. It is amazing how the Lord can lead you. My family and I had come out of established churches. My children used to laugh at me about this little place. I told them they saw what it was then, but the Lord gave me a panoramic vision of what it was to become.

The very things that I said we would do in my acceptance speech is exactly what we have done and is evidence that God was and is in charge of what was and is happening in Broadview Baptist Church. (Refer to my Acceptance Speech.) We have done all that and more. I knew the hand of the Lord was upon me.

My pastor, Rev. Harry McNelty of First Baptist Church in Melrose Park, came over and installed me. It was the first time Broadview Chapel had been the host to that many guests. The offering that day was $750.00. I told the treasurer and the trustee who were so excited over this small amount of money that soon we would have so much money that we would hardly be able to count it.

As I mentioned before, we had a very limited adult membership. I had to call Brother Rorer to the side about different issues relating to church administration and business; he would listen to my suggestions. At that time, Bro. Rorer was a very ambitious man but with worldly views. Brother Rorer was a retired military man. He is now a very fine pastor in a far west suburban town.

He was an invaluable resource during this critical period of beginning to launch this work for the Lord in this new vineyard.

Mrs. Martha Johnson, an original member, and William Rorer had petitioned to constitute Broadview Baptist Chapel to become a full functioning church. They no longer wanted to be a mission. We had begun to grow. Broadview was not ready financially to stand on its own two feet, but I had the faith. I was young then, and I was working a full time secular job as well as putting in an enormous number of hours at our new mission. They had petitioned for constitution before I got here. There was some heated discussion between the pastor of the sponsoring church, the SBC (Southern Baptist Convention) mission director (now retired), Martha Johnson and William Rorer. Johnson and Rorer felt that the sponsoring church pastor and the mission director wanted to pick their pastor with no input from the people he would be pastoring at Broadview Baptist. The Lord had made the decision; it was His will that I would be the pastor of Broadview Baptist Church.

My first secretary was Sis. Rosetta Smith, our current church librarian. We had our first church bulletin the First Sunday in May and have had one every Sunday since. She was very proficient with the production of the bulletin.

Since we were in the Association building, initially, the rent was very low, about $50.00 per month. We also paid $10.00 per month to use their telephone.

Picture this scenario–a new pastor that the Association knew very little about, except they knew the hand of the Lord was upon me. I began to put together the program, which the Lord had given me. Even though this was a new and small congregation, I had to immediately begin making changes. The congregation would sing the Lord's Prayer and the doxology. I told them we didn't need both of them. They were both prayers. I believed God was calling Broadview to conduct His business in the proper manner, decently and in order. Just because it was a custom, it was not to continue if it did not fit into God's program.

Broadview required discipline, with love. 80% of the members were children, 19% were women and we had one man, Bro. Rorer. One of the female parishioners said she felt the Lord had sent me because we needed a pastor who would disciple and discipline Bro. Rorer, and the rest of us.

We had many needs, one of which was a baptismal pool. We had to look for a portable pool with the dimensions of 4'x6'x8'. Bro. Rorer found someone to make it and someone donated us a lining. Prior to our getting the portable pool, we had to go to my former church, First Baptist in Melrose Park, to baptize. This process took away from the cohesiveness of the service.

Then there was a problem with the music department. Our first musician was a young man named Paul Turner. There was no set day or time for rehearsals. I had a meeting with the music department and told them they had to make a decision on what day and hour they would rehearse. We had to have some structure. They decided on Saturday afternoons at 5:00, and it was Saturday afternoons for 28 years. Only very recently have we changed to Friday nights. We had an old upright out of tune piano, but we praised God. When you praise Him and are sincere, God will honor that because of your pure heart.

It is important for the pastor to take a pro-active role when dealing with choirs and music departments. He should define their roles. They are there to offer music during the worship hour. They are a part of the Body of Christ, not a separate entity. They felt that they should have outside engagements or return engagements because another church had visited them. The same was true of the ushers. They had to understand that they were a <u>part</u> of the body and the body functions as a whole. This is a critical issue for pastors to deal with. It is a custom in many churches that each auxiliary works as a separate unit. That is not the way scripture explains to us the structuring of the church. This is tough love for any pastor, but we must follow the guidelines of our Lord and Savior Jesus Christ. We are one body.

The next problem was a problem with the robes. Some members wanted to buy robes and then cut them off because they were too long. I had to explain to the choir members what the purpose of the robe is–to cover one's body. In those early days, the choir would march in after the devotion. That was the old Black Baptist custom. I decided this custom was unacceptable. The deacons would pray and then the choir would come humping down the aisle. Then the preacher would come out of the office as if he was the big Humpty Dumpty or the big dog. That is why many churches have such long services. This is unnecessary and overlapping. The preacher would then have a minister read another scripture, as though the deacon had not had devotion. That person would read a scripture and say a prayer, really pray a sermon. There was all this duplication; everything was a separate entity. It is so difficult to get over to people that the church is one body functioning in unity.

Then there was the problem with announcements. One person got up and made announcements about their department, then, another person repeated the process about their department, and on and on. The church is one body. We only needed one announcer. It is difficult to have people change, but you must conduct God's business the way he wants it conducted.

Next, there was the problem of the treasury. Each department wanted its own treasury. There is but one treasury, and that is the church's treasury I had to practice tough love. God always prepares each of us for the job he wants us to do. Everybody said I was mean. I was not. I just didn't believe in any foolishness when it comes to the work of the Lord.

The Chicago Metropolitan Baptist Association started to tell us we should pay more rent. They started to increase our rent every two or three months. I felt that the reason they were doing this was because when they came to visit or check or whatever they would do as they sat in the back of the church during our services, they noted that we were growing by leaps and bounds and felt we could now be self-sufficient financially. Bro. Rorer and I had a meeting with the Association trustees about this constant rental increase. I decided to put this business issue on the line. I told them, "You all said you wanted to start a mission here. You are bringing the baby (Broadview Baptist Mission) into the world, but killing it before it can grow. My question to you is, "Do you want to kill this mission or do you want it to grow?" One by one they began to say, "You know, I agree with Brother Hopson." They never came back to us about the rent increase issue.

A young pastor must be able to pastor and conduct business. He is responsible for his flock. That is why I say that it is important for a pastor to take a course in business law in order to deal with the secular issues relating to the pastoring of a church. We bought the building from the Association in 1975 after renting from them for about three years.

Of course, before we bought the building, we had many discussions about the Broadview personnel getting into their hair about little things, e.g., children getting items out of the refrigerator. Since the Association members had been coming and observing our growth and getting disgruntled about small things, one of them suggested to me, "Why don't you just buy the building." I said, "We will." And we did.

By now, Broadview had grown and we had several men as members. We met with the Association and offered them $29,000.00 but they wanted $35,000.00. Finally, our treasurer said we should compromise. They agreed to $30,000.00. We had a new church home. The Association moved to Oak Park. We remodeled the building, changed some of the windows, put a nursery in one of the back offices so those workers and children could see and hear the service, and we went to Indiana and bought new pews. I then understood why the Lord had me be an understudy of Pastor McNelty on the building committee. I needed to know this information in my new pastoral duties. We also began our audio and video program. Brother Mitchell Mapp installed our first camera and TV, so that the overflow crowd in the lower auditorium could be a part of the worship service. We were on the move with the new technology.

Rev. John Williams was the interim pastor because the former pastor had resigned to go to another fellowship about four months prior to my coming. He presented me to the congregation. I know the hand of the Lord was upon me because it is said that the prophet prophesies things he does not understand. I said things in that speech that I know the Lord himself revealed to me. Rev. Williams introduced me as the new pastor of the Broadview Baptist Chapel. Let me share my acceptance speech at this time.

❋❋❋

Acceptance Speech of Pastor Clarence Hopson
Sunday, May 7, 1972
Broadview Baptist Chapel

Thank you Brother Williams. This morning I come with joy in my heart and to say to you, the members of Broadview Baptist Chapel, I want to thank you for choosing me as your pastor. I realize that to pastor is not an easy job. There is more to pastoring than meets the eye; to be shepherd over God's flock. It is a great privilege as well as a great responsibility. As I come as your pastor, I humbly beseech you as followers of Christ to support me in all of the Christian endeavors, which we, as a church and as a Body of Christ and baptized believers in this vicinity, should do.

I come as Solomon did when he was made King over Israel; a young boy, he sought the Lord. When the Lord appeared unto him and asked him, "Solomon, what do you want?" Solomon said, "Give me an understanding heart that I might be able to judge between this people; a great people whom thy has made me king over." And I say this morning the same thing. God give me an understanding heart that I might be able to lead this people where God will have us to go.

Now, I am a great believer in the divine providence of God. I mean by this, I don't believe that I am here because you elected me alone; I believe that all of this was the working of the power of God. I had many incidents in my life to lead me to believe this. I don't believe that we are together by coincidence. It is by the divine will of God that you chose me as pastor and I accepted. There will be much work to be done and many mountains and hills to be climbed. But if we are together, we can overcome. We know that in any life there are problems. There will be problems. There will be misunderstandings. But as Christians and children of God, I believe that we can work out our differences as we move God's church forward in this vicinity. I believe God has called us, the people of Broadview Baptist, to a unique ministry in this vicinity. I believe that God is calling us to let a light shine over here where men and women, boys and girls will come to know Christ as their personal savior. We have a great opportunity and we will work together with the Holy Spirit guiding us to bring men in this vicinity to a saving knowledge of Christ. Our community will have a ministry that will stand as a beacon light to those who are lost and those who are seeking a way.

I will strive to be the kind of pastor God will be pleased with in caring for His sheep, for the sick and to help those to find their vocation. You know, we need to have somebody, sometime, give us guidance in finding our vocation in life. Where does God want me to serve? How can I best serve my fellow man? I shall be that shepherd who will give those directions in this community to the glory of God and for the Glory of God.

Also, I hope to build a strong Christian or religious education program in this church so that our children will know why they are children of God and what is required of them as children of God. And, they will also know that God has some promises for them. You see, too many Christians today don't know the promises of God. God does not renege on any of his promises, but if you don't know what the promises are, how will you know how to get them? In our church we plan to have an educational program in which all of our young people will be enrolled. We need you. If you are going to do and be what God wants you to be, you must begin where He says for us to begin, and that is, learn of me.

If we learn of God, our children will be strong Christians. They will not be carried away with every doctrine and wind that comes along. They won't be blown away with everything that comes along and looks pretty when we should have had a strong educational program. We need the adults as well to assist us in making this education program what it should and ought to be. Now, I mean by this, if we are going to have an education program that is worthwhile, everybody will have to work. You must keep in mind that as we work, if you know we need you to help us, and if you don't know, you need to come to learn. So there is no reason at all to stay away. If you already know, we really need your knowledge. If you don't know, we want to share what we have. So, I hope that you will love me as I already love you. I'm going to serve; I'm going to do my best to give you the kind of leadership with your aid and the aid of the Holy Spirit that God will be truly pleased with.

✳✳✳

After having accepted the Pastorate, the church began to grow rapidly. The Lord was truly blessing us. Later on, I had the privilege of speaking all over the State of Illinois in predominately white churches because we led the state in baptizing for 10 years consecutively, which no other Southern Baptist Church has ever done, even to this day.

When we left that church building on 15th Avenue to come to the 17th Avenue address, the number of members had increased to 383. When the Israelites moved, they always had a count. When we move from here we will have a count. Everybody will have to register. From 1972 to March 30, 1980 (eight years) we grew from 40 to 383.

When we marched to the location on 17th Avenue, the Broadview Police sergeant escorted us. I told him, "The policeman and I have a lot in common." The Bible is my gun. We have a lot in common in that the public only wants us around when they want our services. They don't want the police hanging around if there is not a problem–the same with the preacher. The police represent civil law and I represent spiritual law.

I met with the community leaders and discussed our role as a church in the community. The first Christian Education Department was started by me at our original location on 15th Avenue. Since we had outgrown the 15th Avenue location, it was time for the Lord to move us, and he did to the more spacious facility on 17th Avenue. That was truly a miracle, which I will discuss in the next chapter of the book.

CHAPTER 10

FAITH EXERCISED
MIRACLE ON 17TH AVENUE

"Give thanks unto the Lord, call upon his name,
make known his deeds among the people."
1 Chronicles 16:8

I believe the works of God should be made known to his people when the leadership exercises faith. Because of this faith, we were able to move to the 17th Avenue building. In order to help the reader understand these miracles of God, we have to go back to our first church building on 15th Avenue.

Broadview Baptist Church at the 17th Avenue location is absolutely a miracle. Many people do not believe that we have miracles in our modern times, but God still performs miracles now just like he did when he was here on earth. Many people did not see the miracles that Jesus did then, except for the ones that were considered to be outstanding like opening the eyes of the blind, but there were other miracles that Jesus did that the people never saw. As such, I am going to share such a miracle with you now.

We heard that the Messiah Baptist Church on 17th Avenue was for sale and the Lord laid it on my heart that this was where we were going to be. We met with the pastor of Messiah Baptist Church, an Independent Baptist church, a mostly white congregation, and with one of our local realtors. The realtor had misinformed the pastor of the 17th Avenue facility that we were going to give them $300,000 for the property. I guess that is what the pastor expected us to do. Well, we had never seen $300,000. When this did not materialize, the pastor got upset and got in his car and drove off.

The officers and I went back to our old church building on 15th Avenue. They were distraught. I said to them, "Look, don't you give an inch, God has given us that place; that is the place where we are supposed to be." It's not that we wanted to take anything from anybody, but the former church, Messiah Baptist Church, had already moved out to Addison, Illinois. They were gone physically as far as a church was concerned and was only running a small nursery school there, which was not doing very well. Also, the church building was beginning to look a little dilapidated, due to nonuse and the lack of upkeep.

After the former pastor of Messiah left, the chairman of their Deacon Board and officers met with us for negotiations. They were in a financial position where they needed funds because of some bonds that were due. When we met the chairman of their Deacon Board he never took his seat. I assume it was because he thought it would be a short meeting since we could not afford to buy the building. The other members of his group did accord us the courtesy of hearing our offer to buy. Shortly after that, the chairman became ill; God just completely moved him out of the picture. I never saw him again until after we had bought the church on 17th Avenue and were worshipping in it. The other officers of Messiah Baptist did, however, negotiate with us after they got a new pastor.

Although we did not get an agreement with them the day of that meeting, we offered them a $50,000 down payment. (I want you to see the miracle, likened to Jesus feeding the 5,000. I want you to follow the sequence of events.) We had only $57,000 and we offered them $50,000. They were asking $300,000. They did not accept our offer at that time. They did not say yes or no. We went back to our church and our officers asked, "Do you think they will accept our offer?" I had the faith that they would accept it. A leader has to be a person of faith. My answer was "Yes," trusting by faith. Hebrews 11:1 says, "Now faith is the substance of things hoped for, the evidence of things not seen."

One day the telephone rang and one of the officers of Messiah Baptist asked if we still wanted the church. We said, "Yes." That's when the wheels started rolling and everybody got excited at Broadview Baptist. Of course, most people don't know all of the details, and many times it is good that they don't. This is how the Lord works. He lets the leaders know what's going on. They are responsible for leading the people as the Lord directs. We went back to the church and told the congregation that we were going to buy the church and it looked as if overnight we signed the legal papers. There was, however, a long dry period between the time their officers asked us if we wanted to purchase the church building and the time when the negotiations took place when we offered them the $50,000. A pastor has to be patient and teach his parishioners to be patient and watch the Lord work things out in his own time.

This was an amazing turn of events. When I went back to the church building on 17th Avenue, the former church owners had removed all the pews except two small benches in the pulpit. There was a small round pulpit. The choir stand had two pews. Everything else had been removed. There was not a seat in the church for the congregation.

I went back to our Broadview congregation and told them that we needed pews. However, God had given me the wisdom to explain to the people that they would be buying pews for the church, not for themselves. They could not put their names on the pews. I had seen how disruptive this could be because I had seen this in other churches. When people buy a pew and put their name on it, they would say that was their seat. As the shepherd, I was not going to let that happen at Broadview Baptist. Each pew cost $300 each. I told the church members that they should buy a pew. It was amazing; there were Sunday mornings when I would turn in $2,000 from members and Christian friends earmarked for pews, in addition to monies raised during the service. Although this was from a small congregation, the money began to come in beyond our imagination, a miracle.

We went over into Indiana to a company to purchase the pews. (I was eternally grateful that God had allowed me to be a part of the building committee at my former church so I could know of reputable companies to do business with Broadview.) This is where another miracle begins. (Remember we had only $7,000. That was all the money we had after we made the down payment of $50,000.) The pews cost $25,000. When the company installed the pews, we gave them a check for $25,000 and it did not bounce. Remember, we only had $7,000 left after the down payment.

73

We put new carpeting on the floor of the newly purchased church building. When the installers put the carpeting down it cost $8,000. Upon completion of the installation, we gave them a check for $8,000, which also did not bounce. I want the reader to keep in mind, however, that we only had $7,000 left after the down payment. God was working things out for us. It was a miracle.

We enlarged the choir area and the pulpit area. We added three more benches for the choir so it could hold a 100-voice choir. We also extended the pulpit area. That remodeling came to an additional $12,000. We paid the contractors with a good check. Remember, we had started with only $7,000.

I want the reader to see the miracle. We paid everybody. There was no debt in these transactions. All the bathrooms had to be remodeled. The brethren did the remodeling. They did not charge for the labor, but we had to buy the material. I don't remember the cost of the materials. That's also a part of the miracle. We put in a P.A. system that cost us $8,000. I remember this very precisely because it was also a miracle; we paid them their $8,000.

One well-meaning member suggested to me where we could go and get a used piano and used organ for the church. I emphatically told this member, "No." You never offer God something that is secondhand or used. I made it plain to the congregation that as long as I was the shepherd over the Broadview Baptist family, we would never offer God anything used. God wants to be first. The reason I am mentioning this here is because people need to know this. Young divinity students and preachers, especially should be aware that they need to trust God for provisions, and give Him your first and best. Whenever you make God first, He blesses everything. This principle holds true also for tithing. Most folk have not learned this principle yet. I hope the information in this book will be an aid in helping people to trust the living God who is the giver of all things.

Remember, we only had $7,000. We bought a new concert piano and a new organ. We paid $18,000 for them. We did not pay on a payment plan. We paid them in full when they were delivered. I hope you can see the Lord working with his people.

Broadview Baptist Church is a miracle. When you get people unified, you have a force that cannot be stopped. The people lined up behind the leadership of this church, and we marched into the 17th Avenue church building March 30, 1980, which was Palm Sunday. It was said that when we came down the street, we were the only people that had unified this whole community. Broadview is a multi-cultural community of approximately 7,000 people. We had the Chief of Police, my brother who is a minister from Denver, Colorado, and my children from different parts of the country among the crowd of more than 1,000 marchers to the new church. As the scripture says we marched in with a high hand. The fire marshal didn't sit down inside the church because it was overcrowded. I don't know how to guess the size of a crowd, but I was told there was an additional 1,000 persons that didn't get into the church that Sunday. They were on the outside. We had a joyous time. We rejoiced at the miracle that the Lord had wrought.

When we looked at the large throng of people, the officers and I thought this was just a drawing crowd because this was our initial service at our new church home. We thought people would go back to their places and we would have to build up our attendance at our new location. This never did happen. The attendance did not diminish. In fact, in 1982, two years later, we had so many people that we would have them sit downstairs and listen to the service. It is amazing how faithful some people are. As yet, we did not have closed circuit TV of our services at the new location. Later on, as the membership grew, we did have a whole new closed circuit system installed.

The membership continued to grow. In 1982, the Lord gave me a vision of how we could accommodate the large membership by going to two services, one at 8:00 a.m. and another at 11:10 a.m. Because of the growth of the congregation, we led the Illinois Baptist Association in baptizing for 10 years consecutively. We became known across the nation for our rapid growth because we were Southern Baptists and, of course, they keep good records. We had visitors in our congregation regularly asking us what we were doing because so much growth was taking place. Of course, you can't explain God all the time. Folks want you to explain God, but you really can't always do that. You can just tell them that God is moving.

Because of God's moving in the congregation, I have preached all over the state of Illinois. I turn down more invitations than I accept. I have also been the keynote speaker at the evangelism conference because our church had baptized more persons than any other Southern Baptist Church in the Illinois Baptist State Association. I am still active now. I was also one of the pastors on the evangelistic speaking circuit two or three times. I served on the circuit with some very noted pastors in the Southern Baptist Conference. I served with Richard Jackson of Phoenix, Arizona, in Alton, Illinois. Pastor Jackson pastored the largest Southern Baptist church in Phoenix. We shared many experiences. We were both on the program in Alton. Most of the churches where I have been a speaker were Anglo-Saxon churches.

I have also spoken in Wesson, Illinois; Marion, Illinois; and a place called Energy, Illinois. Many times the choir will accompany me and, of course, they ask me where I found these towns; many of them they didn't even know were on the map. I became good friends to Jim Wright, a pastor from Energy, Illinois. I have preached at his church, and he has preached at Broadview many times. I am like his father in the ministry; he calls me many times and asks my advice, and I give it to the best of my ability. I have also spoken at my friend Frank Trotter's church in Marion, Illinois. I have gone to so many places that some I have forgotten by name. This has truly been a miracle on 17th Avenue.

With growth, comes additional pastoral duties. The more people, the more problems–the more problems, the more opportunity for you, as a leader, to increase your faith, exercise your gift and let the Holy Spirit give the guidance. Many challenges came with this phenomenal growth. To God be the glory for the great things he has done.

CHAPTER 11

FULLY EXPERIENCING
THE OFFICE OF PASTOR

*"Woe be unto the pastors that destroy and
scatter the sheep of my pasture, saith the Lord."*
Jeremiah 23:1

Pastoring is an awesome responsibility. A pastor must be prayerful, loving and disciplined at all times. There must be balance in his life. He must be under the anointing of the Holy Spirit to achieve the delicate symmetry of ruling his household and guiding the congregation, which the Lord has entrusted to him. Many times that means he must practice "tough love."

A pastor must not be afraid to take a risk and make changes. As a preacher of the Gospel he must at all times remember that the message of Christ does not change; however, the method of delivering that message could, should and does change in many circumstances. In other words, to keep up with the times, change the method, but not the message.

Most people do not like changes. A farmer knows that if he does not trim the dead limbs off his tree, that tree will not produce fruit. We have discarded many of the rituals of the church that are unnecessary and serve no purpose. We used to have Baptist Training Union (BTU). Many did not like the decision, but the church followed leadership and discontinued it. We moved our training to Tuesday evening. When we would meet for BTU, attendance was meager. BTU was a good program years ago, but it was not and is not appropriate for this present congregation. We have not lost the ministry of training, but that particular program was antiquated. We have since greatly expanded training to a full functioning department, with both day and night classes to accommodate parishioners with various work schedules.

With this change, instead of the handful of persons in BTU, we now have Christian Education training on Tuesday, Mission Education training on Thursdays and Sunday School on Sunday. We have 200 to 300 persons in the Tuesday and Thursday training classes every quarter, and about 975 in the Sunday School classes each Sunday. Classes are set up by fall, winter and spring quarters. In the summer we have mini-sessions in Christian Education because of vacations, etc. We also have a two-week Vacation Bible School (VBS), which averages 900 persons per night; it is a great teaching ministry and mission opportunity.

Let me take you back to let people know what God will do when you let Him control. There are still some antiquated programs remaining in our churches. They may have had some spiritual value many years ago, but are not applicable now. Change was a big issue when I first came to Broadview because it dealt with old Black Baptist customs. We got rid of Men's Day and Women's Day. I had a hard time selling this to the congregation, but God prevailed. We got rid of annual teas and fundraisers. These teas, fundraisers, Men's and Women's Day celebrations were simply programs that were time consuming and caused people to fight among themselves about who was going to do what and how things were going to be done. They served no purpose toward building the kingdom of God. The Lord gave me wisdom to see that it was not profitable nor was it God's will to continue these traditions. God's will for His church was for His people to give of their own money and not spend precious time engaged in fundraisers which take away time that could be used for spreading the Gospel.

Now, in our church, we only raise one offering per service. We have three services per Sunday, and this church lives from those offerings. During the three services and two Sunday Schools, we pass the tray, and whatever a person is going to give the Lord we ask that they give it at that time because we will have no other offerings during the service. Right now we have seven full-time employees in this church. They all get a decent salary out of the gifts that are brought by the members of the congregation. We have taught the people not to beg and have these fundraisers, but to be obedient to the scriptures and give of our first fruits. *(Psalm 50:9-12)*

Let me give you an example of what happened in our church many years ago that crystallized my decision: On Women's Day, the women would traditionally choose a chairperson, a woman who was a new member and knew little about the functioning of the church. Then they would proceed to tear her apart because they felt she didn't know what she was doing. In the early years of Broadview, a woman in our congregation who had a very quiet disposition was chosen to be the chairperson for Women's Day. She was hounded so that had it not been for her husband who was a very strong force in her life, she would probably have left the church. I said, "We don't need this." It would take me all the year to bring peace back to the congregation because of confusion over a Woman's Day program. It served no purpose. We got rid of it. This is one of those dead limbs that most churches still carry only because it is traditional. It has no spiritual meaning and it offers nothing constructive for the future growth of the church. It's just that "we have always done it that way and we will always do it that way." That is a chronic syndrome present in most of our churches.

I realize that my writing this book might not have an impact on many of the traditional churches, although I hope it does, but my real hope is that the next generation of young pastors who come along will stick to biblical principles in this area of church support, i.e., tithing of one's own monies for the support of the church. We must do things God's way. Fundraising brings dishonor to the name of the Holy God. "For every beast of the forest is mine, and the cattle upon a thousand hills. I know all the fowls of the mountains; and the wild beasts of the field are mine. If I were hungry, I would not tell thee; for the world is mine, and the fullness thereof." *(Psalm 50:10-12)*

I know the question now is how can we do this since the church is so steeped in tradition. When we were undergoing this process at Broadview, I would have a staff meeting with each auxiliary and ask them why we should keep them, that is, what were they adding to the cause of Christ. One by one this was a way to weed out the dead branches.

Before we get away from the Women's Day discussion, I would like to talk to pastors. We are afraid to let God lead. We feel that because He called us to be pastors and leaders we have to do everything. We have to try and put our hands on everything and we forget that this is God's church and He has more interest in it than we have.

One year we had a Women's Day program, and a woman in the church decided to exert her authority over the chairperson and proceeded to get a speaker. I had already told them that all speakers had to be approved by the pastor. This woman got a woman preacher to be the speaker without conferring with me, or the chairperson. I told her that this was not her job to do, but mine. God appointed me shepherd, and I am responsible for who comes here to speak to His flock. I had warned all departments that if any of them wanted a speaker they were to see me. They were to give me two or three choices and I would try to get the speaker for them. This is very important, because it makes for good relations between the invited speaker and the pastor. The pastor should know who is coming to speak. It is just good manners. Children should not invite anyone to the home without the head of household's approval. No speaker should be put in the position of speaking at a church where the pastor did not sanction his/her coming. It is just that simple.

I told this sister very plainly that this woman preacher was not coming here to speak because I had invited another lady to come to be the speaker. This infuriated her. She started to spread rumors that the program was not going to be anything. She had raised so much havoc among the women that she had almost convinced me it was not going to be anything. The young lady in charge of the program quit; she was upset. I called her up and told her she had only one week to go, she might as well ride out the storm. She agreed to stay.

On the Sunday morning of that Woman's Day program, I got up, took my shower, got on my knees and prayed the shortest prayer I have ever prayed about a situation of that nature. I said, "Lord, that's your church, those are your folk, and if you don't want anybody there, it is all right with me." I got up, put my clothes on and we drove to church like we did any other Sunday.

Usually, Brother Rorer would be at the church. He was very prompt. He was an ex-Air Force person. He lived right down the street from the church. That particular Sunday morning no one was there. When we pulled up in front of the church my children said, "Daddy, no one is here." I want to show you how God vindicates himself. God does not need my help or yours. I took the keys out of the ignition and got out of the car very slowly. When I got out of the car a member's husband, a man who didn't even go to church, drove up and brought his wife, Mrs. Ruth Harris. We walked slowly up the long steep steps to the door of the church. I put the key in the door and unlocked it. We talked as we went in. By 11:00 a.m., the church was filled to capacity. It was packed.

The woman speaker was Sis. Leontyne Mitchell who said that the Lord has blessed because she had been to Broadview before and had spoken to empty pews. The Lord had showed me that he does not need us to fulfill his program. I was so happy about the 11:00 a.m. service, that I did not expect a large crowd in the afternoon. God had already answered. It was full in the afternoon also. I was happy. I rejoiced for about a month over that because God showed me that he does not need us.

He did not need me or anyone else to put forth his program. That premise has become a daily practice of mine to this very day. I do not go around usurping His authority. Folks worry about many things in the church. I don't get upset. This is God's church. It is not mine to worry about. It is God's business. There will always be problems. There will be relationship problems with husbands and wives, adultery problems, single problems, etc. These are common, ongoing events. People get all bent out of shape, but God has taught me. He has shown me. One thing I have learned is that anytime there is a problem in the church, I am to get on my knees just like Hezekiah and spread myself before the Lord and ask Him how to handle it. Never has he given an answer, which did not glorify Himself.

I am hopeful that the reader will see the hand of the Lord upon me in all of these situations. He guides us through all of these issues we think are so difficult. I am giving you a lot of information on things that happened in a growing church because I don't think they are unusual with any church that is experiencing growth and is doing so by following scripture, especially when so much tradition has to be torn down.

Let me cite another incident. We had a problem with a young man who was in the music department. He was very popular with the members. This man put his resignation on my desk. The members had told him if he threatened to quit, I would beg him to stay. One thing they forgot, I never put my confidence in people. My confidence is in the Lord. I took it to the Lord and asked what should I do. He told me to take it to the staff meeting. I took it to the staff meeting. The clerk read the musician's resignation letter. He had made one mistake. He stated his reason for resigning was personal. When the clerk read it, one of the brothers got up and moved that we accept his resignation. When that happened, everybody in the staff meeting got all upset and became unglued. They wanted to know what we did to him to make him resign. I told them he said it was personal. I did not ask him and you should not either; however, if you want to know you will have to ask him. He stood around the church about three months and had his adversaries to come in to tell me that he would come back if I asked him. I never did. I said I did not ask him to leave and I am not going to ask him to come back. He never did come back. He finally went to another local church in the area. He did not last there very long.

When people get too big for their pants God will always reduce them–be they preacher or parishioner. God will not share his glory with anyone. This same young man had a close relative going around in the neighborhood saying that the church would not be anything without him. I don't know how this person came to that conclusion because he did not even attend prayer meeting. I don't mean that he did not pray at home, but he certainly was not praying with us. God had to show this relative, him and the members that His program could go on without his musical talents. When this musician was at our church, we had a good choir. We were singing up a storm. Some people don't like to rock the boat. I say rock the boat. Every once in a while you need to rock the church's boat because people get content and complacent and just won't act right. This was just another incident that I wanted to share with the readers which shows some of the things you experience when pastoring. I brought this up to let you know when you take the problem to the Lord, He will instruct you on what to do. He told me what to do; I did it and it worked out just like He said it would. It was a little rough for a while because our choir dwindled down to a few members. God, however, always has a remnant. He built the choir back up and it was bigger than it was before. God is faithful.

To fully show you how God had His hand on me and that He is in charge of His church, I need to mention another incident that happened. This one has to do with money. People do steal. All of these things can cause great havoc in the church. When I found out about this problem, I prayed a whole week before I said anything to anybody. I had to have clear and concise guidance from the Lord.

I was given evidence and proof from the brethren that a theft had taken place in the church. I got the information from the bank in writing. I had the information showing the impropriety. I still have it to this very day. I am not going to give it to anyone. The brothers had caught him red handed. I petitioned the Lord as to what I should do. He told me exactly what to do. This was very difficult. I was devastated. I had trusted this person. This was grand theft. It was not just pennies. I prayed. God told me to bite the bullet and move ahead. I called the brother in and also my staff who had done the documenting. He wanted to know when I called him on the telephone, what I wanted with him. I would not tell him. I told him I would tell him when he got there. When I broke the news to him, sweat broke out on him and he resigned. He never admitted it. I was going to ask for his resignation. I didn't have to. He just voluntarily resigned. He was so devastated. We could have caused him to have a heart attack because he was seemingly under so much pressure when the news was broken to him. I don't know what we would have done had this happened. It didn't. What I want to drive home to the reader is how God directed me to deal with these situations. This is all a part of functioning in the office of pastor. You have many happy moments when people come to Christ, but you have to deal with some real business issues as well.

Let's look at the ramifications that could have taken place if we had used man's judgment versus the guidance of the Holy Spirit. If we had tried to sue the person who took the money, people would have been taking sides. Channel 7 and Channel 5 News cameras would have been out here and Broadview Baptist Church would have been only a shell. It was handled so smoothly most of the members never knew anything happened. This was the only time I really got angry about an incident in the church. I was only receiving a modest salary, trying to make sacrifices by not accepting a salary commensurate with my position as a pastor. I didn't mind making the sacrifice. I did not complain. What flustered me was that I was making the sacrifice and this fellow was stealing the money. After he left, the finances skyrocketed. The church, then, gave me a decent salary. It was a beautiful experience to watch God work this salary situation out. I said, "Well, God does work things out when you do what he says." I mentioned these incidents, but there are others, because I want you to know that if you are a pastor or are going to be a pastor, you should always take any problem to the Lord. Don't handle it yourself. It may be rough, but if you get your directions from the Lord it will always work out. If you ask God, He will give you the steps to take and the methods to use. None of these steps were easy. One of the main reasons for writing this book is so people that come behind me will understand some of the hills and valleys we have overcome by leaning on God's directions. We must not get ahead of God.

At this writing, we still need additional full-time employees. Our business manager and counseling minister should be full-time. Since we are in the process of building now, we cannot pay them the combined full-time salary they would need to support them and their families, however it is on the horizon.

Traditionally, Black Baptist Churches have a Pastor's Aid department. This department raises extra money for things for the pastor, i.e., buy him a new suit, etc. I don't believe in this kind of thing. This is an outdated method. The parishioners should pay their tithes and the pastor should be given a living wage so he can go and buy his own suit, or whatever necessities he and his family have need of.

I never believed in pastor's anniversaries, birthdays, and those kind of celebrations. I believe it is a waste of time. I tell all young preachers that God is going to whip the daylights out of them because they spend all that time celebrating. Some celebrate for a week, others for a month. God is not in that. I am just being frank about it. We are not doing the work of God. We are serenading ourselves. Every night they have a different church to come in; some churches have two churches to come in to be on program in one night. They seat the pastor and his wife in a decorated chair (I call it the happy chair). Then, these other pastors say all these wonderful things about the celebrant, and a lot of it is just lying. I call it fleecing the sheep, because when they get through at your celebration, then you go to them and do the same thing. God is not in that. It just sounds good and looks good. When do they plan to evangelize as Jesus commanded us to do in Matthew 28:19-20?

God has brought me through the Chicagoland church circuit, and I have been to enough churches to see exactly what was going on. Then there is the appreciation program for the pastor at Christmas. You see, everything is for the pastor. What about Jesus? What about the lost souls?

The Bible speaks about this in the 34th Chapter of Ezekiel. He talked about feeding themselves and not feeding the sheep. They hooked with their horns and drove the little sheep away and drove them to the wolves. They fleeced the sheep. The weak sheep, who do not have any strength, are taken over by the wolves. God said He is not pleased with the shepherds who feed themselves and not the sheep.

Let me describe those wolves and the weaker sheep. The weak Christians go and join cults because they feel that they cannot measure up or compete with the stronger Christians in the church. Then, we get mad because they go and join the Jehovah Witnesses or the Muslims. These organizations make them feel like they are somebody. That is where we make our mistakes as pastors and leaders. I promised the Lord I would never have a pastor's anniversary and up to this writing and pastoring for 30 years, I have not had one. I have received a lot of flack from some of my fellow clergymen about my position on not having an anniversary. I never had one and God has blessed me. I feel I am scripturally correct in this position.

By the way, the Pastor's Aid did a very good job for me the last time it was in operation. Its last president was Sis. Mary Johnson-Rhingold. It has now gone by the way of the dinosaur. I told them the best way they could aid the pastor was to be a good witness. We spend all of our time celebrating from one end of the year to the other pastor's anniversary, choir's anniversary and on and on. In other words, the church is split up in all splinter groups. I don't know why pastors can't see that. The Bible says we are one body, but many members, and in that one body when one member suffers, all suffer and when one member rejoices, all rejoice.

Another issue that comes up frequently and has to be dealt with is the number of treasuries in the church. In some churches every department has its own treasury, which reports to the general treasury once per month. This causes a lot of havoc with missing funds. We got rid off all of that at Broadview Baptist. We have only one treasury, the church treasury. Also, one anniversary, the Church's anniversary—we are one church. *(1 Cor. 12)*

Again, you change methods, not the message. We must stick with the Gospel of Jesus Christ. That must be our focus. We must evangelize and reach out to the lost world. I am not putting any churches down, but we must not lose focus on saving souls. Have you ever thought about the time and energy used in these celebrations? When we engage in these celebrations, we have to go all over town paying back other churches that have honored our pastor and each of our auxiliaries. Now, when are we going to do evangelistic work? We spend all of our time lavishing the leadership of the church with all of these celebrations; we do not have time to do evangelistic work. When that year is over we start the same thing all over again. When will we have time to reach the lost world? We have spent all of our time praising one another, telling each other about how great we are, and folks are still dying and going to hell. We are not concerned about them because the only concern we have is about the person who is in the leadership position of that local congregation. The Lord gave me that wisdom in this area. God let me see the fallacy in all of this. I have witnessed all kinds of trickery that goes with this kind of thing, i.e., pastors falling out of fellowship with one another if one church does not bring as much money as he brought him or vice versa. Sometimes they had to tip it a little. A lot of things that I know I don't disclose in this book since I am already accused of being a renegade when it comes to these things because I am a non-participant in such activities. These are the reasons we don't have pastor's anniversaries under my leadership.

Now, this is a biggie. When you walk before the Lord and do what He says, he promises to bless you. There is nothing wrong with being blessed, but let the Lord bless you. Some folks can't wait until the Lord blesses them; they go ahead of the Lord and go and get their own blessings. When you do that, you will always step on the wrong side of the road and out of God's will.

I have never asked this Church to give me a raise. The church put me on full time as its pastor in 1978 before we moved to the 17th Avenue building. I was a bi-vocational pastor, which means that I worked a full-time secular job as well as served as pastor of the Broadview Baptist Church. I told them that any church that does not take care of its pastor is cheating themselves; however, they did not have to do anything unrighteous to do it. A pastor can live adequately if the church takes care of him. I happened to work for a company that was very generous with me when I was a bi-vocational pastor. I am convinced the Lord had this particular person in a supervisory capacity over me at that time. I could take time off from my job to visit and pray for the sick and preach funerals without a cut in pay because my supervisor had such respect for the Church and for me as an honest pastor. That was the Lord's doing. He knows who to place where and when.

When I left the company to become a full-time pastor, they gave me a year's leave of absence. I could have gone back, with my seniority, after that year was over, but I never looked back at that job. I am talking about doing things God's way and not man's way. If you do things the way God has ordained and ask him for wisdom to do it and walk humbly before the people, God will bless you. I tell people all the time "You settle for a few peanuts, when you could have the whole bag." That is one of my coined phrases.

I did not get a substantial raise until the fellow we talked about earlier in the chapter left. The Lord gave me a decent salary. Then, all of a sudden the brothers decided to give me a down payment on a house. I sometimes think it was a ploy. I don't know if they meant it or not. I don't think they thought it was going to materialize. They brought the idea of giving me a down payment before the church. I have always been fair. I was never overbearing with the people. Whenever a meeting is taking place that is regarding my salary or other money issues about me, I always excuse myself from that meeting. I told the parishioners that when I was working in my secular job the boss never said to me, "If those people at the church love you so much and want you to visit them in the hospital, why don't they put you on as a full-time pastor and pay you." (I felt sometimes that it was implied.) I wanted them to know they were cheating themselves. It was brought to the church. I left after it was on the table for discussion. I remember leaving the church and going home when they were deciding whether or not to make me a full-time pastor and another time I also left when they were voting on whether or not to give me a down payment on a new house. I have never been one to look over the peoples' shoulders trying to see who voted for me and who did not vote for me. You see, I had a good job with tenure. I did not care whether they put me on full time or not. I wanted them to know, however, that a full time pastor was needed and it was up to them.

People don't understand the workload of a pastor. They make statements like, "The pastor ought to work like I do." They don't realize that if you do God's work and do it well, you work much harder than you do on a secular job. My oldest brother who was called to be a pastor before me told me, "If the people put you on full-time, serve the people, don't be lazy, and just show up on Sundays or whenever it's your time to be at the church." I took his counsel. My wife told my father-in-law that her husband works just as if he was on his secular job, except on his days off. I have two days off just like anybody else. You should be faithful to the Lord.

People used to trust pastors. Now they are getting so they don't trust the preacher because so many of them have given us a bad reputation. The pastor is in a position where he can take advantage of people. He should let the Holy Spirit lead him. For example, a young lady in our congregation came to me for counsel after her husband had died. He left her a great deal of money. I had to counsel her as to what to do with the funds, i.e., investments for her children, etc. I could have told her to give me some of it if I had been a crooked preacher. I also had an older lady whose husband had died and I had to tell her also how to handle her affairs. She came to me because she knew I would tell her right and not try to beat her out of her money. She knew I would be honest. The Bible is so true. It is not just talking It has real meaning. When you see the qualifications of a pastor in the third chapter of Timothy, it says a pastor must not be greedy after filthy lucre (money). He must be honest. That is one of the requirements of a preacher, to be honest. I could have taken part of these two people's money because they were willing to trust me with it. They felt I was trustworthy. Since some preachers are crooked and not trustworthy, people don't trust preachers now.

Anyway, I am talking about trusting the Lord. Let's get back to the house. Some of the women got wind of the brothers talking about giving me a down payment on a house and had figured out how much time I had served Broadview Baptist with no salary and how much time, with a little salary, I had spent over and beyond the call of duty. Armed with this information they brought a proposal to the congregation to buy us a house rather than give us a down payment on one. Here again, I was not present when this decision was made. The woman who read the proposal said if they paid me what they owed me it was more than the price of the house. I had been out in Texas and looked at a house that I liked and had decided that I was going to buy my house out in Texas and let our youngest daughter, who was unmarried, live in the house until we retired. My wife told me she was not going to be paying on a house and not stay in it. She was right. She didn't give me any argument about it, though. Earlier, our youngest son had said to me, "Daddy they are building a new subdivision in this west suburban town and I have seen some houses I know you would like." He took us there, and we picked out a house to buy. We would have bought it anyway if the Church had not. It would have been a struggle, though. We would have had to pay a lot more interest. It would have meant that we would have had to sell some property my wife had in Mississippi, but the Lord intervened. The church bought us the house. Again, during this discussion at the business meeting, I left the church building. I turned the meeting over to the chairman of the deacon board. I went home. I said, "All right, you all decide." They called me up at home that night and said, "Well, they voted to give you the house." I said "Praise the Lord."

We bought the house with a 30-year mortgage. We paid the house off so early in lump sum payments each month that we just couldn't believe it. One of the deacons said he gets happy, even now, when he recalls how each month the Lord would replace that money that they had given me to pay that lump sum each month for the mortgage. He said, "When you bless the man of God, He will bless you." He is right. He said never once did the money go down; each month the finances went up, up, up. He said he almost couldn't believe it. That is what the Good Book says, too, "When you bless the man of God, God will bless you." We paid for that house in four years. I could hardly believe it, myself. I thought it was going to take at least five years. Then the preachers in the community got upset about the house. Everywhere I went people were talking about that house. People I didn't even know came up to me, even in the drug store, and told me that they had heard about the house. They talked about it so much that they would annoy me. I started telling people if they spread the news about Jesus Christ the way they spread the news about that house, we would win the world for Christ overnight.

This is what I want to share with the readers in particular and the public at large: All you have to do is walk with the Lord. He does all the rest. Didn't Jesus say having food and clothes, therewith to be content? *(1 Timothy 6:8)* I have learned to be content with what God has provided.

CHAPTER 12

CHRISTIAN EDUCATION - A MUST

"Study to shew thyself approved unto God, a workman that needeth not to be ashamed, rightly dividing the word of truth."
II Timothy 2:15

I have always known that if I ever became a pastor I wanted to have a Christian Education Program in the church. How can we know the promises of God, the requirements for good Christian living, and the benefits of God without study? We need to know what God is instructing us to do and how He instructs us to live. To live a Christian life is to live a fulfilling life here on earth as well as having a promise of life after death. Christianity is not death oriented, but life oriented. Therefore, we need to learn what God's will is for us and how to properly respond to His will.

When I worked at International Harvester in Melrose Park, where we made large industrial equipment, I noticed that every Friday a group of white individuals would come into the plant to tour. They would have a guide, put on their safety hats and safety glasses, etc., and make their rounds to every department, with the guide explaining each operation in the production areas. I never saw any Blacks in the group. I decided then that if I ever became a pastor I would take the parishioner's children out and acquaint them with the outside world. I would show them how they could incorporate their secular lives with their spiritual lives, and see just how much they were integrated. I know it is important to think of the whole man. I was a young man when I had this experience but all of this stayed with me. Today, we are carrying out this type of ministry.

As I stated before, when I was called to pastor Broadview, I knew that I wanted a Christian Education program second to none. This is how important I thought it was. This was an act of faith.

I was the only teacher at Broadview when we first started the Education Department. I studied. I taught and taught and taught. I looked at other church's departments and finally other people came to join us and brought their various skills. We now have an education department with 12 to 14 classes every quarter. Our system is run on a quarter basis. Each quarter we have 300 to 400 people attending the various classes. Praise God for his mercy and guidance.

We publish a directory from our Christian Education Department entitled "Come Grow With Us." The classes vary each quarter, except for core classes. We feel that Christians grow in different stages: *Help Me* (Birth to Infancy–When you first become a Christian); *Tell Me* (Childhood and Discovery–Impressionable and inquisitive stage when you learn and develop the basics of Christian doctrine); *Show Me* (Adolescence and Irresponsibility–The period usually marked by ambivalence, extremism and resistance); and finally, *Follow Me* (Adulthood and Maturity–A period when self-discipline, responsiveness, responsibility, resilience and resourcefulness increasingly dominate a Christian's approach to life). The goal of the church at this stage is to raise up disciples to go out armed with the truth of God in order to win souls for the kingdom.

Each quarter a list of class offerings is posted on the Christian Education Bulletin Board in the hallway of the sanctuary for all members to see. The courses are set up and referred to as various levels depending on their difficulty and amount of work students are expected to do. Upon completion of classes, students are given a Certificate of Completion. Although these are non-credit classes, occasionally one of the local Christian colleges will have use of our facility for teaching a specific class. The Lord has blessed our congregation so that we have a large number of certified teachers who are also Christians, and they donate their time and talent to our department. This is not to say that a good Christian teacher has to be state certified in the secular environment. We know and are using some teachers in our department who are exercising their God-given gift to teach in our department. Although, we appreciate the training that we give and have been given in the secular world, we know that the Holy Spirit is the greatest teacher.

In our 100 Level Courses, we offer the following classes on Tuesdays on a quarterly basis:

New Members:
Step By Step Through the Old Testament
Step By Step Through the New Testament
Experiencing God
Pathways to Spiritual Understanding
Christian Discipleship
Finance and Budgeting

Doctrine:
Salvation and God
The Son and the Holy Spirit
The Scriptures and Sin
The Doctrine of Sin
Faith, With God All Things Are Possible
Hebrews
Christian Basics
Man in the Mirror

Our 200 Level Courses are:
The Baptist Faith and Message
Making Peace with Your Past
Dealing With the Concerns of Women God's Way
Marriage Without Regrets
The Person and Work of the Holy Spirit
How To Study the Bible
Prayer

Our 300 Level Courses are:
The New Age Movement
The Second Coming of Christ

Our Youth Department for grades 7 to 12 offers the following courses:
Who is Jesus?
Your Life as a Disciple
Today's Media: Choosing Wisely
Stewardship: From a Youth Perspective
Finances

Your Body, Time, Talent

Our Children's Department for grades 1 through 6 offers the following courses:

Christian Education Publishing

Whirlybirds

Jet Cadets

Family Entertainment Network

Bible Drill

Speakers Tournament

We are fortunate to have a large and extensive Media Center as a good resource for our teachers.

Additionally, our Thursday School classes, which are sponsored by the Women's Missionary Union (WMU) are:

Paul's Letters

God's Will For Your Life

Youth Classes

Mission Friends - ages 1 - 3

Girls In Action - grades 1- 4 & 5 - 6

Acteens - grades 7 -12

Brotherhood

Royal Ambassadors

Lads - grades 1 - 3

Crusaders - grades 4 - 6

Challengers - grades 7 - 12

Men's Ministries

We also have an extensive Video Tape Ministry. The purpose of the Video Tape Ministry is to complement the regular Christian Education program here at Broadview Baptist Church. Therefore, a series of videos have been identified and screened. These are offered throughout the year. Following is a listing of the videos that are available. They are various series of tapes by noted Christian authors that we suggest our parishioners check out from our Media Center for encouragement. This is just a sample of the tapes our members are encouraged to share:

The Measure of Spiritual Maturity

Finding Peace In a Troubled World

Keeping Love Alive

Roots to Grow Wings to Fly

The Search For Significance
The Mind of Christ
Building a Healthy Self-Concept
Burnout
Coping with Anxiety
The Principles For Christian Success
The Guilt Factor
Knowing God's Will
Memories
Personality Types and How to Cope
Rekindling Hope
Winning the Race

Although this is a fully established department now, remember the Lord started us out with just one teacher, me. I hope this is encouraging to new pastors who are just starting. We grow as we are obedient to the Word of God.

There are many areas of teaching of which the Christian has limited or no knowledge. At first glance you might feel that a class in budgeting and finance would not fit into a Christian Education curriculum, but it is very important to our living a good life. Many of us do not know that the Lord has a lot to say about money and finances. Christians need to know how to handle their monies, and the Bible has a lot to say about this subject.

Our classes can change. We bring in new classes as the need dictates. Recently, we brought in a new class entitled "Developing Young Men for Christian Leadership." I am the teacher for this particular class. Since we have grown, I am usually a guest teacher for specific classes, when it is requested. This class is designed for young men in this society whose parents have done everything for them. These young men don't want to get married to anybody because they are afraid of the responsibility. This is why it is so hard for the young women to get husbands. Most men are naturally reluctant.

I always knew I wanted to get married, but when the time came to put up or shut up, even I got cold feet. What I am trying to do in this class is to teach young men, that getting married is nothing to be afraid of. I cover how to go about being a good husband, the head of a household and how to go about dealing with various issues related to the married state. When I am teaching, I tell them that I would never want to be unmarried. I know I am now an old man, and maybe I don't need a wife for a sexual partner, but I do need one for companionship. It is important to have someone to converse with. It is said that single people die sooner than married people because there is little purpose or meaning in their lives, and they don't have anything or anyone to live for. I don't know whether or not this is a scientific fact or rule, but many singles just give up. People can die unnecessarily.

We had a member in our church who lived a long time, because she felt her grandchildren needed her. Man needs a purpose to live. That is why this particular class is so important and needs to be taught at this time. I have noticed in our congregation that we have many single young men and women. Some of the young men are simply afraid of getting married. They need to know what the Lord has to say about this.

I have learned a lot about life. This church and I grew together. Many times people wonder why I know so much. It's simple; life is a learning experience. We've had people to come from all over the country to find out what we do here at Broadview Baptist. I can tell them because the church and I grew together; I had firsthand experience. I believe the entire church should have some training on a consistent basis.

When I was studying at Moody Bible Institute, I learned the purpose of the church: bring them in, build them up and send them out. My teacher at Moody called this the educational cycle: "BRING THEM IN, BUILD THEM UP, SEND THEM OUT." We have that motto on our church bulletin today. The general idea is that there should always be constant training in the leadership of a church. I implemented the Teacher's Training Class that convenes during the regular Sunday School hour. Those members of the congregation who feel a calling to teach can have their teaching skills honed in this class during regular Sunday School class time. In other words, it is a class itself. This serves three purposes: 1) prospective teachers are being prepared; 2) it helps the pastor and the church know what is being taught to the congregation; 3) you can find out what the prospective teacher thinks about biblical topics and how they relate that information to their classes. The class is ongoing enabling us to continue training teachers for the ministry.

Some of the members in our congregation now were in my teacher training class when I taught that class at First Baptist Church. Many of those students have gone out into the secular world to teach after completing their college courses at the various universities. One of our students who was a recent college graduate when he came to us at First Baptist in Melrose Park has held several positions as Superintendent of Education in major cities in the United States. He and his wife recently came back to our state, Illinois, and received an appointment at one of our largest consolidated systems in the Chicago land area. And, of course, since coming back to Illinois, they joined our church, stating that they remembered and were always impressed with the Christian Education program that we encouraged.

A church is never overstocked with teachers. This is my method of always having teachers available. Whenever there are absences in a class, the superintendent can always come to the teacher's class and get a substitute teacher for that Sunday. Also, it helps the teacher trainee because when that trainee/substitute teacher returns to the teacher's class, they can share with the class his or her experiences. The class can critique what that trainee did. This is very profitable for the trainee and the other students.

There are three fundamentals exercised by a good teacher, you tell, you ask questions, and you provide work. The last two are good ways to get the student actively involved. It is hard to get teachers to understand that you don't teach lessons; you teach students.

You must be concerned about the welfare of the people that you are standing before. I walk by classes and observe that teachers are just lecturing; they need to get the students involved. I always call this to their attention. Teachers feel because they have prepared the lesson they must deliver it as prepared. We used to call that the big jug pouring water into the little jug. The water is just pouring out because the little jug cannot accommodate all that input at one time. You should find out what your students are thinking, and whether or not they are comprehending. Teachers should find out what their students are receiving from them by asking questions. You provide work to the students to see if they are getting a handle on what you are saying. Feedback is also a monitor. It helps the church root out people who teach doctrines that we do not believe. The instructor must teach sound doctrine. You need to know that the teachers are teaching the true gospel in accordance with the scripture.

Recently, our teachers have been getting certificates upon completion of our Teacher Training Program. We are affiliated with the Southern Baptist Convention. Upon completion of their training, our Director of Christian Education Training sends the grades of the teacher trainees in so that they can become certified.

Even though I had studied in seminary and knew what a Christian Education department should be, in all of my life I had never seen one in the churches where I had attended. We did have a small one at First Baptist. I was the only teacher. I knew it was more than that. I could not sell the idea to expand to that church, but I knew whenever God called me to pastor, I would have a full functioning department.

As you can see, from the information mentioned before, we have classes on Tuesdays and Thursdays. Our Thursday division is called Mission Education. It is supposed to be the classes that teach us how to put into practice what we learn in Tuesday's Christian Education. In other words, it is the "hands on" division of training.

I have always wanted the church people to be exposed to the society in which they live. When I was a younger pastor and we were a smaller church, I took the children to various institutions to learn first hand how they operate. For example, when we visited the Cook County Courtroom, the children thought the courtroom was going to be like television court-rooms. Of course, it was not. It was a totally different experience. I discovered that in every situation, life should be a learning experience, not just in church, but everywhere.

I remember a preacher from my hometown in Mississippi told me of an incident. He said, "There was a young preacher and an older preacher who went to a church institute service together. At that service, another younger preacher named Dickey got up and took up all the time that was allowed for speaking, and the young preacher, whom the people liked and wanted to hear, could say nothing because all of the time was gone. As this young preacher and the senior pastor were riding home, the senior pastor asked the young preacher if he learned anything. He responded that he did not because the other preacher took up all the time acting foolish. The senior pastor said to him, 'You should have learned something; that is, that you should not act like that.'" That is a good principle.

We need to learn from every experience in life, both negative and positive. It has been the Lord's guiding us every step of the way here at Broadview Baptist Church. His hand has truly been upon me.

CHAPTER 13

THE "BEGAT" SYSTEM

"Abraham begat Isaac; and Isaac begat Jacob;
and Jacob begat Judas and his brethren."
St. Matthew 1:2

Just as scripture records the biological genealogy by using the phrase "begat," Broadview uses that same system to encourage the growth of our spiritual family. Each member, when he or she is saved, is encouraged to go out and witness to someone else who is unsaved and bring them to the church to hear the Gospel message. Our prayer, of course, is that the Holy Spirit will draw them and they will be an addition to the Christian family of God. Therefore, each one should beget another one.

We preach so that we can bring others to Christ. That is the purpose of the Church. New pastors and church leaders have to be mindful of members of the congregation that say that the church is getting too large and engage in talk about how it was when the church was very small when they knew everyone by name. These members should be shown in the scripture that our mission is to add to the Church. It is God's job to provide space for them. He will. *(See Acts 2:47.)*

When Broadview Baptist first began, it had mostly young people and we used the "begat" system very effectively. I realize the word "begat" is outdated, but we still use it for our purposes; the function is the same. In the first Chapter of Matthew, this was how the world was repopulated. We must repopulate the world with Christians. This is stressed to the new members, i.e., use the begat system. This is very effective for church growth when it is followed.

It is easier for a small church to grow than for a large one, because, in a small church everyone has something to do; in a large church everybody thinks that somebody else is doing it. This same thing applies to witnessing. In a large church the parishioners think that the unsaved will come anyway and nobody has to witness. After a while, if this position is taken, the church membership will die out and everybody will wonder and ask what happened. The "begat" system is a powerful system. If everyone applies this principle the church membership would double every year.

I am not against small churches. I do feel, however, that a church should witness. It's okay for a church to start out small; if it does not grow, however, there is something wrong. The church should grow. If church folks say that they are a small family church and they want it to stay that way, then they have forgotten the mission of the church. We must not forget the true mission of the church, which is to go out and witness and bring others to Christ.

A small church need not stay small. If it is evangelizing, it should grow and it will grow. When we started out, I was not trying to build a big church. I always felt that 800 people was enough for one shepherd to pastor. God had to show me that I had the wrong concept. As we grew God gave me insight and let me know that it is not the intention of ministry to limit the size of the congregation, but quite the opposite–it should grow. As long as there are unsaved folks, the church should grow, i.e., you should continually win souls for Christ. It is our job to tell the Good News. If the people hear the Good News and the Holy Spirit draws them you will need more room. It's simple arithmetic. God will provide the room if we witness.

Our church motto goes hand in hand with the "begat" system. You bring them in (you evangelize them), you build them up (you teach them) and you send them out (so they can evangelize others), and so the cycle of new birth continues. It is a process of coming and going. That is why we call the first cycle, the cycle of evangelizing, and the second cycle, the cycle of indoctrinating and the third cycle is to go out and do it all over again. I learned this process when I was in seminary. It has worked very well for our church and it will work for any church that uses this principle.

CHAPTER 14

A GOING CHURCH FOR A COMING CHRIST

*"Behold, I come quickly: blessed is he that keepeth
the sayings of the prophecy of this book."*
Revelation 22:1

Although we do not know when the Lord is coming back, we do know that He is coming. We are to be busy witnessing until He comes back. Broadview Baptist Church is a Going Church for a Coming Christ. The Holy Spirit works in every believer.

As I stated in the previous chapter, during my first year at Moody Bible Institute I took a class in Christian Education and the professor drew on the blackboard the education cycle. A light came on in me; Bring Them In, Build Them Up and Send Them Out. I wrote this down and never forgot it. The Holy Spirit does not always tell us everything right then. I would later use this at Broadview Baptist Church.

The inscription on our Church bulletin is "A Voice of One Crying in the Wilderness, make straight the way of the Lord." The Lord gave this to me long before I was pastor. When He gave it to me I wrote it down and kept it in my pocket. Later on, one of our deacons did a painting for me on this subject and it hangs in the hallway of our present building. When I became pastor, I implemented it as our church bulletin inscription. The scripture reference is *John 1:23*.

We enter the church to worship and leave to serve. That is to say, that when you come into the church doors, you are entering to worship the Lord, but when you leave, you are entering the mission field to serve. That is why we have this on our doors upon entry and exiting from our church building. This is a gentle reminder to the parishioners.

Again, we come to the house of the Lord to be refilled so we can go out and serve. The analogy that I draw here is it is just like going to a gas station to get gas; you get your gas and go on your way. You do not get your gas and just sit at the gas pump. Our statement over the door is, "You are now entering the mission field; be fruitful and multiply." While you are in the field, you are to multiply and bring others to Christ.

A pastor has to be careful when using these statements, because they can be misunderstood, especially if there are unchurched people in the audience. When we first put the statement, "You are now entering the mission field; be fruitful and multiply," up on our front and rear door, it was misunderstood by some. A lady came up to me and said she thought it meant to go and have more children. I explained to her that in this instance it had reference to adding new members to the family of Christ.

Since we are a going church for a coming Christ, we need to use every resource that the Lord blesses us with in order to get the message of Christ over to the unsaved, as well as to preach the Word to edify the saints. To that end, Broadview Baptist has been blessed to have an assistant pastor and a number of associate ministers who serve with the pastor. As I mentioned earlier, the pastor does not have to do everything himself. He is responsible, but he does not have to do everything personally. A good pastor needs to know how and when to delegate.

A case in point: after our church body had grown and the Lord had sent so many other laborers in the vineyard to help at our Church, I found that it was important that I allow these new ministers of the Gospel the opportunity to exercise their gifts. As a church grows a pastor needs to know when to let go of some of the responsibilities and let others help with the work. *(See 1 Cor. 3:9.)*

Many times a pastor feels that he must preach every sermon at every service. Why do you think the Lord sent you help? You should rotate your assistant pastor and associate preachers, not only so they can exercise their gift, but also to relieve you of the necessity of preparing two to five sermons per week. It also allows the congregation the opportunity to hear other speakers and give you the opportunity to make sure that the true doctrine is being preached by the minister. In the process, you are blessed, the congregation is blessed and the new associates are encouraged. As the Shepherd, you also have the opportunity to give constructive criticism in sermon preparation.

As a result of this process, eight pastors have gone out to full-time ministry from the Broadview Baptist Church. They are Jimmie Daniels, Frank Gibbs, William Rorer, Marion Morris, Tony Pierce, James Nailing, Brad Traywick and Charles Pearson.

After all, remember that someone gave you a chance. I am forever grateful for Rev. Thomas of Pilgrim Rest Baptist Church and Rev. McNelty of First Baptist Church for allowing me the opportunity to exercise the gift that the Lord gave me, that is, to preach the Gospel of Jesus Christ.

We must be about our Master's business disciplining laborers for the harvest. This whole experience, too, is a blessing that the hand of the Lord was upon me in giving me the wisdom to help others. *(James 1:5)*

CHAPTER 15

THE MINISTRIES OF THE CHURCH

"Thou wilt surely wear away, both thou, and this people that is with thee: for this thing is too heavy for thee; thou art not able to perform it thyself alone."
Exodus 18:18

As we witness and teach, people are saved and the numbers increase. Inevitably, we need help executing the various items on the Church's agenda. The more people you have, the more problems you have. These problems, however, are our opportunities to see the Lord work. Since our congregation grew from having only one Christian Education teacher to having a Christian Education Department, it also expanded from my being the only person to counsel parishioners with various problems to a full area of counseling ministries. We try to address the whole man.

As I stated before, I hope this book can be used as a teaching tool for young ministers. I hope they look at the historical progression of events to this point of development. It is critical that a proper spiritual and administrative foundation is laid in the early years of a young congregation.

The following ministries are active in Broadview now; there can be additions or deletions as the need arises:

College Scholarship Ministry
I am particularly proud of this ministry we have for our youth. The College Scholarship Ministry has been blessed by God ever since I have been pastor. We have been able to take the graduating students out to dinner each year. The whole church body participates in this dinner. This is the only social event that we have. Once per year we will all go out to encourage the graduates and have a pleasant social gathering outside the church building. The Scholarship department has grown so much that

each year we not only take the 8th grade graduates, the high school graduates, the various college graduates out to dinner, but we also give them monetary scholarships accordingly. We give out scholarships twice per year; once in the fall and once in the spring when the next semester begins.

We give scholarships according to the needs of the student. Our budget last year was $45,000; we had about 28 graduates. We do this to encourage them. The bulk of the monies go to the students who cannot afford to pay the tuition to go to college. We ask that the students keep at least a C average. We also send them a love and encouragement "home-away-from-home" gift basket of goodies during the year to let them know that their church is still thinking of them. At Christmas break, these same college students do Christmas caroling at the various senior citizen homes in the area. We want the students to be mission minded always.

Counseling Ministry
The Counseling Ministry is one of the most extensive ministries we have. It is an umbrella ministry that encompasses the Grief Ministry, the Drug Ministry, the Divorce Ministry and others. If the problem comes up we tackle it, but it is headed by the Counseling Ministry.

The Grief Ministry is one that we have to be very careful with. We have to be careful because we have to know when grief is supposed to end. In the scripture we found that people grieved for 30 days and then went on about their business. The danger of some of our ministries is that it can make the members lazy, make them more dependant rather than independent. We have to monitor this carefully. Since I am the overseer of the flock, I must remind the ministers who are over various ministries not to allow the members to become too dependent. The object of counseling in the grief ministry is to make the person whole and independent again.

We also have the Drug Ministry, which is called Substance Abuse Ministry. As an older minister, I get on the young ministers about the name of this ministry. I feel they should just call it the drug ministry and not soften it up by calling it substance abuse. I think that we rename and sugarcoat names to make them more palatable to us. The minister in charge said the reason this term, substance abuse, is used instead of drug is because there is more than one kind of substance that can be abused, i.e., alcohol. I concurred. They meet every Friday night. I share whole sessions with them sometimes. Not only is Minister James Shannon present at these meetings, but also another minister and a trustee function as facilitators. Often they bring in speakers whom the Lord has freed from the habit of using illegal drugs and alcohol. Many people are freed in this Friday night ministry from the grips of drugs and alcohol.

Hearing Impaired Ministry
We have been in this location on 17th Avenue for about 22 years. When we were in our first location, we had a young man in the congregation who knew sign language and asked if he could interpret the service. We had only two deaf members at that time, but the services of that young man were needed.

We still maintain a group of trained signers and use them in all of our services. We do not know how many members or visitors who come to our church are hearing impaired. We are just here to serve and make sure everybody who comes into our church is exposed to the Gospel of Jesus Christ. We do not segregate the hearing impaired in the congregation. They sit with everyone else. Our program is inclusive, not exclusive.

Hospitality Ministry
This is one of our newer ministries. My wife is a part of this ministry. The first impression people get of a church starts in the parking lot. They check to see if everything is neat, grass is cut, etc. Therefore, the parking lot attendants, the ushers and the hospitality persons play a very important role in making people feel comfortable. It's important when guests come to the church that we make it our business to speak and be courteous to them; we should even have light conversation, prior to talking to our friends and our buddies, because we want the guests to feel comfortable and welcome. We say we are a friendly church and I believe we are. I make it my business to try to shake hands with and greet all visitors that come to worship with us. This is important because a new person to the community can easily feel unwelcome if no one engages in any friendly verbal exchange with them when they are at the church. They can feel isolated. The Hospitality Committee tries to erase those feelings of isolation.

The Hospitality Ministry is new and growing. Remember, we must be innovative; we must go forward and meet the needs of the people. We can't stand still; if we do we will become stagnant. Any pastor who is satisfied with the status quo is not going to succeed in the ministry.

We must always look for new methods and means to reach others for Christ. That is the purpose of the church. God mandated us to "go into all the world and make disciples." That is what we must keep in mind. I don't have a problem with this. I came out of the era of segregation. I am an African-American. The hand of the Lord is upon me. The Lord raised me up in segregation and protected me in all of that; it does not cause me discomfort to reach out to my Caucasian and Hispanic brothers. When I walk down the street and see a man lying in the gutter, I say to myself, except by the grace of God that could be Clarence Hopson lying in that gutter. What I mean by that is that God loves that person. As long as that person is alive, God loves them.

Legal Ministry

Our Legal Ministry is headed by one of our young lawyers, who is also an associate minister here. He is almost overloaded. He is here long hours counseling with members. His job is to help people with legal problems who are unable to afford an attorney.

I might add here that the church also has a lawyer on a retainer. When I first came to the church, I told the congregation that we would always have a church lawyer on a retainer basis because it is necessary to have one to handle any legal issues that come up in the operation of the business dealings of the church. This attorney (the head of the legal ministry) is not here to represent all the members on a free legal basis. He can, however, give limited general advice to members before they see an attorney, or he can tell them whether or not the issue requires an attorney. This is free advice unless he is hired by the member to handle his case. We are a church, we are not in the legal business.

Library/Media Ministry

We have a full-functioning Library Ministry; we are in the process of renaming it the Media Center Ministry. We have a head librarian who is excellent and is used by the Southern Baptist Convention sometimes to help train other church librarians. Our library is run on a similar basis as the regular public library. We use the Dewey Decimal System. We have a staff of persons who work with the head librarian. Our library has designated hours. Members can check books out. They are given a library card that they can use whenever they need to.

I think it is important to let you know how we got started. When we were a small church we asked members to place a book in the library in honor of a loved one. Many of the members did. We had our beginning. I personally gave five books. My mother was the mother of four sons who are preachers, so I put a book in the library in honor of her; also one for my mother-in-law, one for our oldest daughter and one for my father, etc. This is a way to start a library in a small church. Also, some schools were changing their books for whatever reason and they helped us out by giving us appropriate books.

Our librarians are all accredited. We also have the syllabi of all the various Christian Education courses that we teach here as well as films and videos of all worship services.

Nursery
The Nursery is upstairs and is part of the Sunday School during the Sunday School hour. When the regular worship service is started the audio and video ministry makes sure that the department can hear and see the service. We have trained nursery attendants and teachers for the young babies and toddlers that are housed in the Nursery Department during the worship services. These regular nursery attendants and junior nursery attendants enjoy working with small children. Because our church is large, we have two rooms dedicated to the different age levels with age appropriate toys, i.e., Bible stories, games and other memorabilia available. The children that are old enough to sit quietly and listen to the sermon can because the Video and Audio departments make sure that service is available to the students and the teachers. I learned much of this by being exposed to the Southern Baptist Convention methods of operation.

Nurses Ministry
We are blessed at Broadview to have trained professional nurses who are seated at various areas in the congregation so that if any medical crisis

arises and members need assistance, they are there to provide that assistance until the paramedics arrive.

Publicity Coordinator/Announcer
This ministry is responsible for making announcements during each of our worship services. They are also responsible for making sure the appropriate announcements are printed in our weekly bulletins. Although we orally announce things, we also print them in the bulletin so the members can take them home. They are also responsible for making sure that our special programs are announced in the local newspapers.

Security Ministry
This group of men direct people to the various parking areas. They also use large umbrellas during rainy weather to walk women to their cars if they are parked far from the church. They have a rather large staff that covers the four full services that we have on Sundays and Wednesdays. The Bible says we are one body, but many members. All of these various ministries serve in diverse capacities so that the total ministries work smoothly. Since some of the members of this ministry are members of the civil police department, they also accompany the finance department in transferring funds to the bank.

Shut-In Ministry
The workers in the shut-in ministry come out to the church every week and send tapes of the Sunday's message to all the shut-in members. If the shut-in has a VCR, they send videos; otherwise they send the audio tapes. Many of our parishioners have told us what a blessing this ministry is to them when they can no longer get out to the house of prayer physically.

One of our young ministers who was in Saudi Arabia during the Desert Storm War said it was a real blessing to attend Broadview Baptist Church services by video out in the desert during that conflict and told us how it blessed the many soldiers.

Telephone Ministry
Some years ago we developed our telephone ministry We have six booths equipped with telephones, and the basic function of this ministry is to keep up with members who have been absent for a number of days and/or weeks.

112

The church clerk, who keeps the membership records, gives a printout of the missing members to the telephone ministry worker. (They get these records by the process of deduction. Each member is asked to fill out an offering envelope at least once per week that he or she is in attendance–there is a special place on the envelope for checking off "attendance only.") If there is no envelope filled out that member's name is listed on the printout. The member does not necessarily have to give a gift to complete the envelope for attendance.

Upon receipt of the printouts from the clerk by the telephone ministry, we approach this job with a spirit of humility and concern. We let the person know that we miss them and are concerned about their spiritual and physical well-being. We record the responses. This information is passed back to the clerk and is monitored.

This is also an outreach program in that every person who answers the phone may or may not be a member of the Body of Christ; if not, we can share the Gospel with the respondent.

We keep accurate membership records. Each month the clerk gives me a detailed count of the current membership and how the changes occurred, number of members active, number of members delinquent; number of members added from other fellowships; number of members who left by default or by letter or other means; number of members baptized; the number of members that died. We have the whole count in order to keep our membership files current and active. The telephone ministry relies on the clerks for this information.

Usher Ministry
This is a very important ministry in that they are responsible for seeing that people are seated comfortably as they come into the sanctuary. They are also standing guard to watch over the congregation to make sure any needs the members have during service can be handled in an orderly fashion. They must assist in emergency situations, along with the nurses, in case of illness or any disruptions. They are the quiet workers that are the doorkeepers in the house of the Lord.

At Broadview we have a Senior and Junior Usher Board that graces each of our worship services in the main auditorium, the lower auditorium and the upper auditorium, when needed. We have more than 80 ushers to work in the various services. They are rotated so that no one usher is overworked, but fresh to do the work assigned to him or her. This is one of the largest ministries at the church. It also has one of the largest Junior divisions. It is sorely needed. Many times they have to assign special ushers for funerals and home going services at various times during the week. They also take charge of handling the flowers during funeral services, and sometimes have to act as pallbearers.

<u>Van Ministry</u>
This ministry is a vital part of the hand of the Lord being upon us. Many people wonder why we go and pick up people and bring them to church. We have three vehicles. These are large modern vans; one is equipped to handle wheelchairs.

When people want to come to church, they call the church and our van drivers pick them up. Many people feel that if people really wanted to come to church, they would get their own ride. This, however, is a very important outreach. We try to indoctrinate our van drivers. When we get in the new facility, we are going to have routes. If you want to come to church, you just have your sign in the window or stand at a specific location and the van will pick you up. This is part of the wisdom that God has given me. The hand of the Lord is upon me. We will have the north route, the south route, the west route and the east route. Each bus will leave in the morning and the evening to pick up people for the services. There will be four different regularly scheduled routes. Many people who ride the buses are our regular evening service worshippers.

It really bothers me that people don't understand that their responsibility is to obey the commands of the Lord. We tend to want to do what we want to do and not what Christ commands us to do. If we don't like a particular program or choir that's singing, we won't come back to the night service at the church. It's all about what I like, not supporting God's program.

If you are only interested in what you want you have not grown in Christ, you are like a babe in Christ. A baby only wants what he wants; he cries when he wants the bottle and sucks his finger if you don't give it to him.

That is the way some of our Christians are, spiritually, I mean. They say they only want to go to Church once a week, but you don't go for yourself. The very fact that we are out here is saying to the world that we love Jesus. Jesus said if you wanted to follow him, you would have to deny yourself. If you deny yourself, you don't do what you like, you have to obey.

When are we going to learn that following Christ doesn't give us any other option but to obey? If we don't, this means we have not completely sold out to Christ. When we accept Christ, we die to self. It is every Christian's responsibility to witness. We must make Jesus known to the unbeliever. We must witness to everybody wherever contact is made. They don't have to listen. You don't have to get results every time. But, it is your job to witness. Again, I repeat, we must make Jesus known to the unbeliever. This is the beauty of being a Christian.

<u>Video Ministry</u>
We have been blessed to attend the Southern Baptist Convention every year since 1974. My wife said she would always find me in the Video Department whenever we went to the convention. I would go to that department because God had already given me a vision to know that our church was going to grow so much that we would need to know how to operate a video ministry. I know the hand of the Lord was upon me. My wife and son didn't know about the vision. The Lord gave me the vision, not my wife and son. However, now they understand. We started with the black and white video in the original church building on 15th Avenue. Now, we have three studio cameras.

Our younger son heads this ministry; people get the videos and take them all across the country. I mentioned earlier the career military man, who was also a minister from Broadview Baptist. Upon receipt of his video from home, he started to watch our sermon during the Gulf War Conflict. He looked up and he had a large group of soldiers enjoying the service in his tent. That thrilled my heart. We were spreading the Gospel of Christ to our servicemen in Saudi Arabia.

The Video Ministry director has a staff of about 22 people because we have three services here every Sunday and we have to use six people at each of these three services. We have three on cameras, one monitoring, several monitoring the studio and one downstairs with the headset. A lot of people don't like to go downstairs to see the service on closed circuit TV. It is a substitute, in that they do not see the pastor, choir and officers in person since we don't have the seating capacity in the main auditorium for all the members. Our goal is for people to hear the Gospel. Some people will not go downstairs because they feel they are just watching TV. Some simply go back home. This is one of the main reasons we are building a new church facility, to accommodate all of our people. Many have not matured to the point that they understand that ministering to the person does not have to be in person. We must remember that we should utilize whatever is available to us in order for the Gospel message to go forward. Some members, however, enjoy the downstairs auditorium with closed circuit TV. Remember, many of the early Christians had to receive the Word by letter.

A church should never get so big that it does not have the family touch, spiritually speaking. We still have the family touch. The individuals worshipping downstairs with the closed circuit follow the program along with the members upstairs. Because the communication is so good with the video ministry, when the bread and wine is presented, we all eat and drink at the same time. They sing, take communion, offer the invitation, etc., all along with us. We communicate via headset. I make sure I stand at the head of the stairs to shake hands with the members when church dismisses so that they still feel a part of the church family.

The Video Ministry plays a great role in the church, not only while we are ministering, but also after we leave the church. Our Video and Audio ministry makes copies of the services and they are sent all over the country to different ones as well as to the sick and shut in. If members want to purchase a copy, they pay $3 for the audio and $5 for the video. This is the cost of the tape itself; we do not charge enough to make a profit from them. The church purchases the blank tapes. We sell the tapes to the members for the same price that they cost the church. In other words, you are reimbursing the church so we can purchase more tapes for others so they can avail themselves of the service. The Gospel is not for sale.

Also, when we go out annually for the Graduates Dinner, our members pay for their dinner only; we do not inflate the prices so that the church

116

makes a profit. God has blessed us. I believe that God will bless a church that loves and is a giving church. We are a giving church. I know the hand of the Lord is upon us because I have been told that it wouldn't work and couldn't work and it won't work, but it has worked and it is working. I always remind the church attendees that if they go to a church and have to pay to get in to hear the Gospel, the Lord is not in it; the Gospel is free.

Recently, we got a letter from a person in Memphis, Tennessee, who is not a member. He said that our message via audio and video was a real blessing to him. He even sent us a financial gift for our groundbreaking. The Bible tells us, "Cast your bread upon the waters and in many days it shall return to you." That is what we must do. The church must cast her bread upon the waters; we cannot afford to operate like the world.

WMU (Women's Missionary Union)
The WMU is the missionary training ministry. We have Girls in Action for the young ladies and Brotherhood for the young men. The Girls in Action trains young ladies how to be mission minded at an early age. The Brotherhood trains young men how to offer service to the shut-ins, and function as hosts when visitors come to the church for various meetings. The young men's group is called the Royal Ambassadors.

Others
We have a family day program at our church annually. Each year we have a coordinator for that program. It is a day of fellowship to bring the entire family together in worship.

Additionally, we support the Cook County Jail Ministry by supporting the salary of a chaplain there. Financially, we also support our Illinois State Baptist Association (ISBA), both locally in the Chicago area and statewide in Springfield. And we give to the Potter's House, Children's Home, Moody Bible Institute, Mt. Sinai Drug Baby program, and other programs in the community as the needs arise.

Our Church Training Director is full-time. He oversees the Tuesday Education Department, Mission Education Department (Thursdays), Sunday School, Teacher's Training Class, etc. He is responsible for all training at the church.

At this writing, we have Department leaders for the following departments: Announcements, Audio, Chapel Choir, Church Anniversary, Church Training, Counseling, Deacon Board, Deaconess Board, Discipleship Training, Family Day, General Auxiliaries, Hospitality, Impaired Ministry, Junior Choir, Library, Male Chorus, Nursery, Nurses Board, Publicity, Sanctuary Choir, Scholarship, Security, Sunday School, Telephone Ministry, Treasury, Trustee Board, Usher Board, Vacation Bible School, Van Ministry, Video, WMU, Youth, and Youth Choir.

Some of these departments are ministries within themselves, therefore, you will note some overlapping in the names.

We have, at this writing, 1 assistant pastor, 12 associate ministers, 37 deacons and 11 trustees.

CHAPTER 16

THE NEW CHURCH

"Where there is no vision, the people perish..."
Proverbs 29:18

The shepherd must always look out for the sheep. He must always be looking for better grazing ground for the sheep. When we were in the smaller church building on 15th Avenue, we were looking for the larger site on 17th Avenue, our current, second home, at this writing.

In 1982, we went to two church services. I realized then that the growth was going to be larger than the facilities we had. The two services did not suffice because we had to have closed circuit television. Many people will simply not watch closed circuit TV. Some people feel if they have to watch closed circuit, they may as well stay at home. We always have to think the way the carnal mind thinks in our planning because we must do whatever we can in order to reach those persons for Christ. A dedicated Christian will watch the closed circuit and be inconvenienced a little bit, but a carnal person will not.

In building a new church, one of the most important things a pastor should realize is the necessity of adequate parking space. Again, the unsaved and casual Christian will not bother to look for parking, they will say "next time." We have to make parking convenient to the worshippers.

Fifteen years ago the Lord gave me the vision of this new building that we are getting ready to go into and I told the officers about it. The officers told me about a young man who could put my vision in a composite drawing. I met with this gentleman and told him what I saw in the vision and he attempted to draw what I had described. The first time I went to see his composite, it was a beautiful building. However, I told him, that was not the vision that I saw. When God gives you a specific vision as to how something is to be done, you must not accept anything else. I told the architect that he had neglected to put the dome in the drawing. He drew another, with a dome, and I told him that was not what I saw in the vision either. Then, I gave him some more information. He did the drawing the third time and I said, "That's it." I received a correct drawing from the young gentleman for the new church in July, 1987.

When building a church, it takes time, patience and much prayer. When we got the drawings, we had to get the property. We started to negotiate with the Navistar Company which had 17.9 vacant acres for sale. God takes us through phases. We thought we were going to be at 17th Avenue and 22nd Street where Navistar had 17.9 vacant acres in addition to their improved acreage. If we had gotten that land we would not have had to tear down a building, as we had to do on the land that we purchased at 25th Avenue and Roosevelt Road. Navistar wanted to sell their property as one parcel, which was the vacant and improved land totalling more than 100 acres. We did not need that much land. We only needed about 7 acres; so we negotiated for the 17.9 vacant acres. The village preferred that Navistar sell it to a profit making mall in the area. We felt that we got cheated out of the property. K-Mart got the area and they wanted us to bless their endeavors. How could we bless a place that we thought we were supposed to have. We had to use faith. God was still with us. We followed the Bible and we just allowed God to bless us.

In searching for a place to execute this vision the Lord had given me, we negotiated for one year with a company called Allied. It is a subsidiary of an English company. It was a slow process because we were doing negotiating with a European parent company. That culture was not working as fast as we would have liked. We started the negotiations in 1995.

God prepares us for negotiations. I realize how important it is not to rush God, but to listen to his instructions. Many of the things I learned as a part of the Building Committee as a young preacher at my former church are beneficial to me now. God knows what He is doing.

Four officers of our Church and I met with the mayor and his aides about the Allied property and unknown to us, two other companies had tried to get the property and failed. If God has something for you nobody can take it away. The mayor had given them a tax write-off to aid their buying the property. The companies were unsuccessful. I guess the mayor felt that if those two companies couldn't buy the property, neither could this little Baptist Church. However, when the hand of the Lord is upon you, you will always make the right decision.

The mayor said we had to get a special zoning permit and he would help us with a special variance permit. There are three kinds of zoning permits, namely, commercial, industrial and residential. The village said that the property in question was in an industrial zone. The mayor agreed to assist us in our endeavor, but, during this process, we had to go to court. The Lord knows how to put people in positions when He is getting ready to execute His program. We had a contact person that had worked for Allied and was familiar with their parent company in England. Information was faxed to and from England. Allied was asking $6 million for the property. Then, they came down to $4 million. We offered them $800 thousand as a final offer. Our attorney said we should offer a little more. We agreed and offered them $999 thousand for the property—just short of $1 million dollars, and they accepted. When the hand of the Lord is upon you, you can't lose.

Because there was asbestos on the land, the Allied Company gave us a check for $200 thousand for its removal. All of this happened by the divine providence of God. Otherwise, we would have been responsible for its removal. Putting the gentleman with the Allied connections on the committee was important. Also, having our Church Training Director and Church Business Manager on that committee was equally important. This team was critically important in our negotiations. I know some of the members did not like the way some of the negotiations were carried out, but the people, in some instances, didn't like Moses and God. There is nothing new about differing opinions or techniques on how business is carried out. As long as God is pleased and we are following his directions, that is what really matters. Those who worked closely with me knew that the hand of the Lord was upon them and me.

I had to make some unpopular decisions in this process. It took real courage and determination and a willingness to bypass personal feelings to secure an architect who was not a part of the Broadview Baptist family. We knew from talking to our architect who was in our congregation that this project was too large for him. He knew it, too. As an African-American pastor with a predominately African-American congregation I had to take some heat for going to a large white Wheaton Architectural firm for our final product. I could not, however, let racial preferences shade my good basic business decision. It is my responsibility to look out for the sheep.

Another reason I am writing this book is to let young pastors know that you have to make hard business decisions and sometimes they may be unpopular. However, if you do what is right, the Lord will bless you and honor that decision. This is imperative, not only for pastors, but also for any person in a leadership role in the church. Finally, it was a unanimous decision to get the Wheaton company to be our architect, because their firm was the best for this project.

There is a lot to this process. Let's go back to the village and the judge for a moment. The judge told the village that they were unfair to us because today people travel for miles to go to church. Most churches build in industrial zones. We went to the village zoning committee and they gave us clearance. The village started to give us clearance, but their attorney said we had to have the property rezoned. The mayor had to break a 3 to 3 tie vote; he voted against us. I was terribly disappointed. Our attorney asked us if we wanted to sue the village and I said, "Yes." The truth is the light, and the lawyer pursued it. I didn't know that you had to go through so much. We had to give depositions. I answered the questions and told the truth. In the meantime, we moved the asbestos from our newly purchased land. We spent a lot of money. When the hand of the Lord is upon you He provides everything you need. This is a fact. To the reader, I say, if the Lord has given you a vision, stick to it, don't give up and don't get weary.

We had the asbestos removed and then demolished the building, which was the tallest building in the Village of Broadview. This whole process reminded me of when Nehemiah was rebuilding. The Sanballat personalities came telling us what we should have done. They said we should have gone to the village first before buying the land. Many other things were said during this time. We cleared the land. We had to go to court again. The Village was giving our committee a hard time. We had to stay prayed up. How could people on the outside looking in know more than the people, the committee, that is, who was handling the project.

We had some internal discord just like Moses, who had to deal not only with the enemy but also with the people he was leading. Some of them wanted to get a party and go back to Egypt. God let the land swallow up some of them. When God gives you directions and says you are going to the promised land, that is where you are going, even though you may lose some along the way.

I am grateful that the hand of the Lord was upon us. Prayerfully, we all agreed that we, as a committee, and as a church family would stand together. God has and he continues to bless us.

We went to court. I was the first and the last on the witness stand. I was like Jesus, I was the first and the last. The first time I was on for 1 hour and 20 minutes. The hand of the Lord was upon me and I was able to answer all the questions sufficiently. God gives you favor with some people. I believe God had given me favor with this judge. The village attorney asked some irrelevant questions. The judge chided her for that. She was curious about the finances of the church and the architect assured the judge that we were very able to handle the building of a church of that magnitude. The judge felt the architect was the expert and accepted his statement as fact.

When I got back on the stand the last time, I was the last one. The village attorney had a list of all the money we had spent and read it all off. We had already spent $2.5 million dollars. She wanted to know how much we owed. I said we didn't owe anybody a penny. The judge raised up in his seat. I hate the fact that we had to go to court, however I enjoyed the learning experience of watching our judicial system in action.

Let me reiterate, every pastor should take a course in business law if he plans to operate his church well administratively. He must be at ease with legal terms. Of course, the village appealed. The village wanted to hold the building project up because they did not want us to build. The case was taken to the Appellate Court and the decision was upheld so that we could build. The judge gave us permission to build. We invited the mayor and his staff to our groundbreaking December 1997. The hand of the Lord is upon me. I praise God for this. I am glad the Lord allowed me to be an apprentice in Church building at First Baptist Church in Melrose Park.

I told the brethren that in order to be on the Building Committee, you will have to burn some midnight oil. I have a plan for us to build debt free. I shared this plan in the business meeting. Whenever I get a revelation concerning something about 2 or 3 o'clock in the morning, I know that is the Lord talking to me. God has never given me a plan where He did not provide for its execution. When I made my presentation at the Church's Business Meeting, I asked that I not be interrupted until I had finished. If members had questions during the presentation, I asked that they write them down and I would address them at the end of my speech. My presentation was understood and accepted; there were few questions. I know we will have to sacrifice, but we can build our church debt free. This plan that the Lord has given me is fair and we will have more than enough finances to carry out this program.

Monies that we give to the mortgage company in interest is money that could be going toward the ministry. The scripture says that the borrower is servant to the lender *(Proverbs 22:7b)*. That is one of the reasons why we want to build debt free. Also, when you offer God something, there should be no other strings attached to it. That is another reason for debt free construction. God has given me some very specific visions about the physical layout of the church we are to build. You must remember this vision was 15 years ago. We will have water fountains in specific locations. At the new location, we will have a 25th Avenue entrance and parking lot entrance with fountains that spurt water six feet in the air. The water will drop back into the pools. The baptismal pool will have continuous running water. The hand of the Lord is still upon me.

When you give God something, you should give Him your best. I think the church has cheated God and given the world a reason to beat us over the head by giving God hand-me-downs. We give the world the idea that God is so poor He cannot sponsor His own work. That is an insult to God because He is the creator of all things and everything belongs to Him. *(Psalm 50:10-12)*

Back to the new church building. In the ceiling we will have a dome with 500 starlights shining. The seating capacity will be 2,200-2,300.

The balcony will be situated so that when the alter call is given the people can easily come down to the invitation area. There will be a 240 person choir stand and a 30 person orchestra pit. Additionally, the choir will have a 250 person rehearsal area. This will be a mechanized area so that a button can be pushed for this area to come in and out of the wall. I don't believe in giving God any hand-me-downs. You have to make God's house attractive.

Jesus said, "I make you fishers of men." When He says that, He means for us to use our gray matter to study how to catch the fish. You are not going to catch fish unless you have some bait to attract the fish. You are not going to go there and just whip your pole out into the water and expect to catch fish. If you are going to catch the fish you have to have something to attract them. The church building is the attraction; but when the people come, we are going to give them the Gospel of Jesus Christ.

We will have a lighted dome on top of the Church that can be seen afar off. We will be a physical as well as a spiritual light in the community. We will be able to park 600 to 700 cars in the parking lot, with ample parking for the handicapped. We estimated that would be about 3 people per car. We will have minimum street parking. We will have an area for a 2nd deck for parking growth, if needed. Our entire building will be totally handicapped accessible. Our chapel will seat 250 people for weddings and funerals. It can also accommodate a small choir. There is also the possibility of buying property around the church. We'll have approximately 40 class and media rooms.

A note of importance to young pastors reading this book is the necessity of having input from your department leaders in the planning stages of building a new church. We may not be able to give them everything they want, but they should be able to let their requests be known so accommodations can be made for them as much as is feasible.

We will still have two worship services at Broadview Baptist, and of course, Sunday School each Sunday morning. We expect an average of 5,000 people for worship on Sundays. We will be able to host the State Conventions and will be a hub for the Chicago Southern Baptist Convention. We will have dressing rooms on each side of the baptismal pool. Our cameramen will be on a catwalk. I had the vision of the seating arrangements in the new facility so each person will have a good seat. In addition, we will have 10x9 built-in screens.

We have over 30 different ministries and are continuing to grow. We cannot maintain the status quo. Anytime a church does that, it starts to die. A church has to be willing to give and lose herself in the work of the Lord. Jesus said, "He that loses his life for my name's sake shall find it." The church has to keep implementing programs as the needs of the people compel.

We are not building a new church because we need a building per se, but we build so we can more adequately serve the people. The church is in the community for a reason. It is there to offer God to the community. The question we need to ask ourselves constantly is, "What would Jesus do?" How would He deal with these day to day problems?

Of course, you get tired, as a pastor, because you are giving attention to so many different areas in the church, but this is the calling of a pastor. Sometimes the members say I am a little tough, but I have to do what I have to do. I have to tell the truth in love and love people beyond myself. When I say that the hand of the Lord was upon me, I have to give the glory and honor to God. The pastor has to give himself away. Even my youngest son said to me one day when we were driving along in the car, "Daddy, I pray for you daily. I don't know how you deal with all those different personalities with everything you have to do." He does not know this, but that touched my heart deeply. He is a young man. I told him, "Well, Son when God gives you a job, He gives you the means to deal with it." I don't know myself. We have a congregation of nearly 3,000 people. When you count the people in the community whom we serve that are not members of this congregation per se, it is more than 3,000.

This brings up another important thing. If a church is in the community and its only concern is its own members, it is a dying church. If any church caters to its members only, it is a dying church because the membership will diminish and before long it will die out. You must always reach out into the community and constantly bring in new people.

The church's mission is still to bring lost souls to Christ.

CONCLUSION

"Let us hear the conclusion of the whole matter: Fear God, and keep
his commandments: for this is the whole duty of man."
Ecclesiastes 12:13

One of the reasons for writing this book is to aid young pastors in the
ministry. I want them to grab the truth of God, trust Him and walk with
Him.

Many pastors have asked me to tell them about how God has blessed our
church in many areas. I always share whatever information I have with
them. There is too much to do in the Christian community to hold back
information from our brothers and sisters in Christ. It has been said that
only 25% of the people in the Church are saved. We have another 75%
of the population to preach to, witness to and serve. In addition to this
population, we have the many people who are unchurched that need to
be preached to, witnessed to, and saved. We don't need to compete for
church members–there are enough unsaved and unchurched people out
there that need the Gospel. For this reason, I always like to share the
totality of my experience about my walk with the Lord. I want people to
know that they can have the same, or an even greater walk with Him.

In my prayer every morning, I ask God to let me be a blessing to
somebody. One of the things I have learned since I have been here at
Broadview Baptist Church is that even though we preach the Gospel, our
Sunday School and the various training classes are merely intellectual
exercises for some of our parishioners. It seems to be insufficient for
people when they have troublesome lives. This training is not meant to be
just psychological stimulation, but instruction in a walk of faith. People
seemingly come unglued when life's problems come upon them. This is
a real concern to me. I am not saying that people should not cry when they
have problems, but they should not fall completely apart. Another of my
favorite scriptures is, "God is my refuge and my strength, a very present
help in trouble." This is found in *Psalm 46*. I emphasize "in trouble"
because in this life you will have trouble. It goes on to say, "Though the
earth be removed and the mountains be carried into the middle of the
sea...." I want the people to grasp these truths. I want people to under-

stand what God is saying. If he says nothing is impossible, He means that absolutely nothing is impossible to those who believe. I want the people here to seize the full essence of this. I want them to really understand that God will do what He says He will do.

Let me reiterate, whenever a person is fearful, he is telling God indirectly "God, I do not trust you." He wouldn't dare just come out and say that. He is saying, "Because I can't trust you, I am going to be overwhelmingly afraid." That is what people do. When I talk to them, I try to tell them this. David said, "Though I walk through the valley of the shadow of death, I will not fear." God is in control. Believers need to know that nothing, absolutely nothing, can happen to them outside the permissive will of God. God allows things to happen to us. God doesn't do it. Take Job for an example. God allowed things to happen to him. The devil did these terrible things to Job, not God. Many times calamities come upon us to be a blessing to someone else. Sometimes these experiences are to make us strong; sometimes they are to bring someone to Christ. Many times God allows us to lay up in the hospital for six to eight weeks in order to bring our roommate to salvation; or He brings the pastor in to minister to them while you are there. If the pastor had not visited you in the hospital, they might not have heard the Gospel message. If Christ died for our sins (and He did), then we should and ought to be willing to suffer whatever to bring others to Christ.

Remember, every person is important to God. We have to take the attitude that it is not God's will that any should be lost. We can't pick a bad sinner or a good sinner. As we go into the world, we should preach the Gospel to every creature. We must let the Holy Spirit guide us to witness to whomever we meet. I don't say that we must witness to every person we meet. We must be led by the Holy Spirit. That is our mission. Sometimes, believers complain of hurt feelings following attempts to witness. We are dead in Christ. We have no feelings. Whatever any person does to us he is doing it to Christ. We are reflections of Christ.

In Christ's hand you are safe. Nothing will happen to you. Paul says that God does not give us anything that we cannot bear. He gave Job the strength to bear it. He allows you to get in those unusual situations in order to strengthen you or to bring someone to salvation. When unbelievers observe our Christlike behavior in an unfavorable situation, they are curious to know what makes us so focused and calm during these hardships. They see you standing strong amid this condition and that is when you can witness to them and tell them about the Lord. The greatest witness in the world is for people to see how you handle yourself during trials, situations in which the natural man would crumble. Perhaps, it is the death of a child or a relative, etc.

Now that I have grown old in the ministry, I don't talk much about these things with my peers because their ways are established, but I do try to tell the young men in the ministry. Many of us preachers have a good whipping coming because we have played the harlot. We have violated God's word. That is why we have no power. We are trying to carry out God's program without the Holy Spirit, and that is why many of us are impotent.

When people get up in Prayer Meeting and testify, they usually talk about something material that the Lord has blessed them with. I think they should start off with the known and go to the unknown. I think this is an area that needs growth. We need to talk about what the Lord has done in our spiritual walk. Most of our testimonies are of something physical that we have received and it does not go any farther than that. We need to testify of the spiritual things that the Lord has done for us also. There is nothing wrong with a testimony of the physical or material things, but Paul, who was very well educated, who sat at Gamaliel's feet, said he counted it all as dung for the knowledge of the excellency of Christ. This is what I like to hear in our testimonies. Things that we see in this life are going to perish; things that we see are transitory; they are going out of existence; the only thing that is eternal is our relationship with Christ. That is what I hold on to. I try to convey this in my sermons and my teachings, as well as my Christian walk.

The Christian should live in expectation of Christ's return. We are the bride of Christ. A bride that is not with her husband is always graciously awaiting the day when she can be with him. That is the way Christians should be. We are looking for the day when there will be no more problems, no more sickness, etc. We are looking for Christ's return. But, we are content with the here and now. Pastors condone too much secularism in the Church by not warning the people of His return.

Many pastors allow the people to use them and worship them in various celebrations. This is human nature; people always like to worship something that is tangible, something that they can touch, and that is why they worship their pastor. He is the one that is praying for them. They can see him. When God blesses them, they say, " Rev. Hopson prayed for me and I got well." I constantly remind them that I am just a vessel. I want them to see Jesus. He is the one that heals. People get the idea that they can get around giving God the credit by giving accolades to the preacher, who is tangible. Many cannot grasp this truth. Let me give you an example: the children of Israel. Moses was on that mountain only 40 days. It amazes me that Aaron was so weak that he let the people talk him into making that golden calf. How can an inanimate object that's man made help you in the time of trouble?

In the Book of Jeremiah, they cut trees out of the woods and set them up in their houses and bowed down to them. How can you worship something that you made? The object is never greater than its maker. They weren't satisfied with God; they said "This is our God." They knew that the image had not brought them out of Egypt, hadn't dried up the Red Sea or brought water out of the rock. God got angry and was going to destroy them, but Moses prayed for them. Praise God for someone who stands in the gap and prays for us.

We need to let our children know that the Lord is the One who delivered us from slavery, from the plantations, from Jim Crow and from past hard times. <u>We must let our children know that the Lord delivered us.</u> We try to hide this from our children and pretend we have been in Chicago, or wherever, working in plants and offices all along. Even in Chicago, you had segregation in certain sections. I had to learn that there were ethnic neighborhoods. All the problems were not just in the south. Before affirmative action, we had difficulty in the north getting jobs and promotions, also.

God used our Caucasian brothers to help bring us out of that plight. That was and is God answering the prayers of our ancestors. For example, even when we went to get a loan, it was difficult and we were charged exorbitant interest rates. We paid twice the interest of our Caucasian brothers. But, God brought us through that. We paid it and God blessed us. Because we suffered, it has been much better for our children. Many of our children don't know this because we do not tell them the story. We hide it from them. Our children need to know that we came through great hardships with the help of the Lord. In this area, we could take an important lesson from our Jewish friends who never let their children forget their deliverance from slavery in Egypt, even though it was hundreds of years ago.

I have been accused of not being interested in voting and politics. This is untrue. My wife and I were registered voters in Mississippi before the Civil Rights Act was passed. We have voted continuously. We voted before the Martin Luther King era. We were members of the NAACP, which was the leading Civil Rights group at the time. We had to pay $2 poll tax in order to vote. We lived in Jackson, Mississippi at the time, which is the Mississippi State Capitol. During the Civil Rights Era, the poll workers would try to disqualify people by asking them crazy questions like how many bubbles were in a bar of soap. Of course, the Black people did not know how many bubbles were in a bar of soap and neither did they. In some places you could not vote if you did not own property. Most Blacks did not own property at that time and they knew that was just a tactic to keep them from voting.

This is what bothers me now. The greatest privilege citizens have is the right to decide who governs them in this country. We are unaware of the many people who have died in order to give us that privilege; not just in the Civil Rights Movement, but prior to that, it was the Women's Suffrage Movement (white women). They paid a great price to be counted. It has not always been just the Black folks. It was the women, too. We must make our children aware of these things. It has not always been like it is now, and even now it is not as it should be. If we sit back and start lying down on the job, the ways of the past will return. I try to get people to see this. I encourage them to vote.

By the way, I still have my voting papers from Mississippi. We were in district 55. I didn't destroy them. When we came to Chicago, I registered to vote immediately. When each of my children became 18 years of age, they all registered to vote. I instilled in them the importance of the ballot. These are the kind of things I want to pass on to the readers of this book—just to show how God has worked in my life.

As I said before, I got my higher education under the G.I. Bill. God's hand was on me when I was in Mississippi. His hand was on me in Illinois. When I moved to Maywood, there was only one Black family in our block. We made friends with our neighbors. Most of the white neighbors died out. They did not run. The world is constantly watching Christians. I had a beautiful lawn, but if it did not get cut on Saturday, it would have to wait until Monday, because Sunday is the Lord's Day. My neighbors said they had watched me and observed that if my lawn was not cut by Saturday, it would not be cut on Sunday. This, too, is a witness. Your neighbors are watching your conduct. We think we can do anything on Sunday, reasoning that it doesn't make any difference. Yes, it does. God is a peculiar God. It amazes me how in the Old Testament God was so very specific about putting the blood on the tip of your finger and on your ear lobe, etc. God is specific and particular about how we are to do things.

God says, "Remember the Sabbath Day to keep it holy." Another thing many people have not noticed is that the Bible does not name days by alphabetic notation. They are identified by numerical designation, not by such names as Monday and Tuesday. The Sabbath was the seventh day. Sabbath means a day of rest. We call Sunday our day of rest. When people insist that Saturday is the Sabbath, we go to the scripture because it is our basis for our decisions. I have discussed this with Seventh-Day Adventists. I say that the Bible says that six days shalt thou work and on the seventh thou shalt rest. The seventh day for us is Sunday. Jesus said the truth shall make you free. We let tradition control us. Many of us say we can go fishing or do whatever on Sunday, but God says we should keep the Sabbath Day holy.

Some time ago, I let the politicians have a forum in the basement of our church on a Saturday. The people thought I had changed because I said politicians could not speak here. I meant then, and I mean now, they can't use the pulpit on the Lord's day to conduct any political business. That is the Lord's day. However, I cannot divorce myself from politics. That would be ludicrous. Even if we want to have a Vacation Bible School parade, we have to get permission from the politicians. I want to influence people who have some Christian principles, therefore, I must be interested in the political arena. However, it must not be first in my life. God must be first at all times. There was some disagreement with my position by one of the deacons who said I could just say to the congregation, "At the end of the service on Sunday, anybody who is interested in hearing from the politicians could just stay after service." I shut him up with the Word of God. Jesus said, "Remember the Sabbath Day to keep it holy," not the Sabbath morning. This is why the pastor needs to know the Word of God gives us a day of rest because we need it. Many of us leave church and go somewhere else, instead of going home with our families. Some of us go so much we don't even know our children. To prove this point, God even let the oxen rest one day. God said even your land needs to rest. I am not a farmer, but my dad was. Every seven years, the land was to rest. If you plant the same thing in the same ground, you will get less and less yield each year because you need to turn it over and change the crop. If God rested, you know man needs to rest. The Sabbath is for two things, worship and rest. We need to make our children aware of that. That is why the Legislature passed the Blue Law to keep businesses closed on Sundays so people could get some rest. It would be good if the malls were closed on Sundays. We should only have drug stores open on Sundays for emergencies.

I have been blessed to live in one of the greatest centuries of discovery known to man. I don't know what happened before the flood, but the twentieth century has been the greatest century for discoveries since the flood, as we know it. We have experienced most of our industrial and technological advances in this century. We have gone from the T-Model Ford to the Concorde with supersonic speeds. It is the Lord who has brought us to this point.

Let me say here that it is critical for a father to spend time with his children. Your first responsibility is to your family. God holds you accountable for your family, be you pastor or layman. You would be surprised at what children remember most. It is not the gift you gave them, but the time you spent with them. My children tell me they enjoyed my taking them on long drives, buying them ice cream cones, etc. They remember our Friday night "griping sessions" where every member of the family got a chance to air their opinions.

The main reason for writing this book is not only autobiographical, but it is to let people know how the hand of the Lord was upon me. It is also to show how the Lord led me into the leadership position of this church. I wanted to share our experiences with other young pastors, preachers, students and the public at large, showing how the Lord leads. God is still in the guidance business when we walk with Him.

The Bible says that the just shall live by faith. In fact, recently, the Lord gave me that message to preach on a Sunday. I got real excited. That is another thing, I think the minister should let the Lord give him His message. God should determine what His people are to receive, not the minister. I wait for God's direction on what to preach each Sunday and I work as hard as I can to deliver what the Lord gives me to give to his people. We don't know the needs of the people. That is why we need to seek God's face for guidance in sermon preparation. Even when I have felt my sermon was not sufficient, a parishioner would come to me and say, "That was just for me." That is a confirmation that it was indeed God's message.

In conclusion, I hope the reader can see the hand of the Lord working in my journey through life.

I am an old man now, but as I reflect on my 70+ years, I see that God has been faithful throughout my entire life as I yielded my life to Him. During my military tenure, my years as a young husband and father, as an evangelist and pastor, God has been faithful. I am especially grateful for His answering an early prayer I prayed when I was a young preacher. It was my desire that His people be taught the Word. He has honored my request and I thank Him. We have one of the finest teaching and educational programs in any church. I am eternally grateful to the Lord for allowing us to teach the true Gospel of Jesus Christ to His people.

As we set our sights on our new church, it is with a humble spirit that I ask the Lord's blessings upon this congregation that He has entrusted me to shepherd, and the entire Broadview community both now and in the coming years. We want to remember not to become complacent and self-centered because of the blessings that God has bestowed upon us.

Amen.

Pictorial

Clarence W. Hopson's Graduation Day from Moody Bible Institute, May 11, 1971

The Rev. Clarence W. Hopson has been elected pastor of the Broadview Baptist Church, 2001 S. 15th Avenue, Maywood.

Rev. Hopson for the past eight years has served as an associate minister of the First Baptist Church of Melrose Park. He is a graduate of Moody Bible Institute.

The Rev. and his wife, Ann, and their five children, Priscilla, Wilbur, Denise, LaVerne, and Jeffrey reside in Maywood.

Announcement from local newspaper upon the election of Rev. Clarence Hopson as Pastor of Broadview Baptist Church

Graduation of Priscilla, oldest daughter, from Mary Holmes College,
along with Annie and Pastor Clarence Hopson

Denise, 2nd daughter, being escorted down aisle by Pastor Hopson
on her wedding day. She was being married to Byron Brown.

Blessing of 1st granddaughter, Maya Brown

(left to right) Marvin Craig, Priscilla Craig, Denise Brown, Pastor Hopson (holding Maya)

Hopson family at wedding of youngest son, Jeffrey
(left to right) Denise Hopson Brown, LaVerne Hopson, Pastor Clarence Hopson,
Maya Brown, Annie Hopson, Angela Hopson (bride), Jamarah Craig,
Jeffrey Hopson (groom) Priscilla Hopson Craig, Wilbur Hopson

Rev. C. W. Hopson and two fellow ministers at Illinois Baptist Convention, where Pastor Hopson served as Vice President of Illinois Baptist Pastor's Conference

Pastor Hopson offering the invitation to discipleship at Broadview Baptist Church's worship service during his early ministry

Pastor Hopson attending to administrative duties in his office
as Pastor of Broadview Baptist Church

Broadview Baptist Planning Conference being moderated by Pastor C.W. Hopson

BBC Planning Team are left to right Trustee Marvin Harris, Rev. Marion Morris, Pastor Hopson, Rev. Tony Pierce and Deacon William Morris

BBC Fun Time at the Annual Church Picnic. Jeffrey Hopson (Pastor's son) with two other youthful members of Broadview Baptist Church–Mr. & Mrs. Vincent Dodd

Annual Vacation Bible School Parade
"We Shine For Jesus" was the theme for that year

Broadview Baptist Church's 30th Anniversary
Cutting of Anniversary Cake by Pastor and Sis. Ann Hopson

Pastor Hopson congratulates Mr. & Mrs. Pitts after performance
of their marriage ceremony

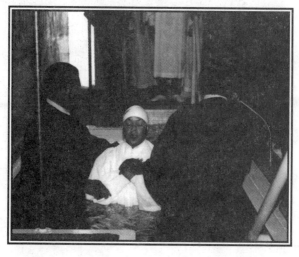

Baptism at BBC by Rev. Burlock and Rev. Pierce; overseen by Pastor Hopson

Broadview Baptist Church's First Home

2001 So. 15th Avenue, Broadview, Illinois 60153

Broadview Baptist Church's Second Home

2111 So. 17th Avenue, Broadview, Illinois 60155

Broadview Baptist Church Groundbreaking Services, December, 1999

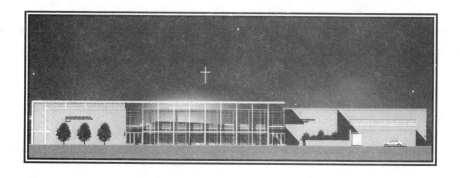

Broadview Baptist Church's new home on 25th Avenue
at Roosevelt Road, Broadview, Illinois 60155

Mrs. Annie Hopson and Pastor Clarence W. Hopson